WARRIOR
GODDESS
WISDOM

D0647807

Also by HeatherAsh Amara

Awaken Your Inner Fire

The Warrior Goddess Way

Warrior Goddess Training

The Toltec Path of Transformation

WARRIOR
GODDESS
WISDOM

Daily Inspiration for Women

HEATHERASH AMARA

Hierophantpublishing

Copyright © 2018 by HeatherAsh Amara

All rights reserved, including the right to reproduce this
work in any form whatsoever, without permission in
writing from the publisher, except for brief passages in
connection with a review.

Cover design by Emma Smith
Cover art by Elena Ray
Interior design by Frame25 Productions

Hierophant Publishing
8301 Broadway, Suite 219
San Antonio, TX 78209
888-800-4240
www.hierophantpublishing.com

If you are unable to order this book from your local book-
seller, you may order directly from the publisher.

Library of Congress Control Number: 2018957306

ISBN: 978-1-938289-80-4

10 9 8 7 6 5 4 3 2 1

Printed on acid-free paper in the United States.

For all the women on this beautiful planet.

INTRODUCTION

The book you are reading now is the fourth in the *Warrior Goddess Training* series.

That being said, I want to be clear that reading any or all of the first three books—*Warrior Goddess Training, The Warrior Goddess Companion Workbook,* and *Warrior Goddess Way*—is not a prerequisite to receiving the full benefits of the teachings in *Warrior Goddess Wisdom.*

As you will soon see, each page contains a bite-sized nugget of inspiration that is easily accessible for all women (and also highly recommended for men as well). There is no right or wrong way to be a Warrior Goddess; so whether you are new to the process or a seasoned Warrior Goddess veteran, I welcome you.

The mission of the Warrior Goddess movement is to help you transform into who you are meant to be, by going on a deep journey within. As you progress on the Warrior Goddess path, you will cultivate two aspects of your inner being: a fierce Warrior focus and commitment, and the compassionate Goddess faith, receptivity, and creative flow. This newest guide, *Warrior Goddess Wisdom*, offers a simple and direct way to integrate these teachings into your daily life, and will help you take your Warrior Goddess journey to the next level.

Our path is one of reflection, compassion, and perseverance, and I ask you to keep these traits in mind as you look inward and begin to deepen your self-knowledge and self-support. As Warrior Goddesses, we are learning to shift our attention away from how we think we are supposed to be in favor of finding out who we really are at the soul level.

I hear from many women who have big dreams (or even small hopes) and are frustrated because they can't seem to reach the goals they've set for themselves. They have a sense of what is possible and a yearning for change, but they find themselves responding to and managing the chaos of their days, rather than carving a clear, creative, and focused path for themselves and their future.

With the unlimited challenges that hook our attention every day—emails and texts, busy work and home lives, social interactions, not to mention the sudden emergencies and unexpected surprises life can toss at us—it's all too easy to get derailed and find ourselves exhausted and disheveled by the end of the day. How do we stay on track? How do we hold our focus?

This is why *Warrior Goddess Wisdom* is so essential. This mini guide will serve as a compass to help you stay pointed in the right direction, and focused on your own inner desires, dreams, and destiny. Each page offers a simple daily practice that contains a quote, a short reflection, and a daily action or mantra. These passages are designed to guide you back to yourself, to help you seek your own answers, and to explore your inner knowing. Your own deep wisdom will be your best teacher and friend on this journey.

How to Use This Book

Let this book be a guide and a friend that is always there when you need extra support and direction. Feel free to do one meditation a day for the next few months, or allow yourself to be surprised by randomly opening to any page and seeing which message is waiting for you. You don't have to do the meditations every day, though there are wonderful benefits to creating a self-care ritual that includes setting an intention for your day. Maybe it's taking as little as five minutes each morning for yourself to ground in following your chosen path, which will make every subsequent step easier to manage.

By the same token, it's important not to overwhelm yourself with these exercises and ponderings. They may be short, but they are mighty, and the lessons shouldn't be rushed. I recommend that you read no more than one or two reflections at a time, or they will begin to lose their potency. Each page offers you an opportunity to go within and reflect on that day's teaching and how it applies to your life. If you try to rush through to the end, or read large chunks at a time, you will miss the medicine that has been created just for you. This is not a "hurry and get to the end so you can check it off your list" book. It's a book that gently guides you as you become more sustainably committed to a daily practice that will nourish you in the long run.

The same recommendation goes for those who are prone to overthinking. Rather than looking for "the one" meditation that you think you need, try one of the above methods of choosing one to read (sequentially or randomly) and focus on discerning how the lesson of the day could apply to you. Some of the daily meditations, at first glance, may not seem to be "for you" and they may even make you uncomfortable, but it is those challenging or seemingly non-applicable writings that will support and invite you to explore yourself more deeply. In doing so you may find that there is something to be healed that you have been avoiding, or that the teaching can be looked at in a different context or perspective, which makes it relevant to your unique situation. The deepest wisdom doesn't come from what our minds already know, but from seeking deeper meanings and truths in the unknown.

I suggest setting aside a specific time each day to read the quote and meditation, and then sit quietly and savor the words. Imagine that you can slowly digest and assimilate the concepts and wisdom, and absorb the nutrients of each sentence. If you have time, you can journal the thoughts and insights that arise for you throughout the day. Or pick one word or concept from a daily teaching and use it as a core focus for that day.

An exercise, mantra, or other form of invitation follows each writing and is designed to guide you as you continue exploring the concept throughout your day. Some of the days will have an action for the day and some will have a mantra. Each action is a short question to ponder or an experiment to try. The mantras are short phrases for you to take with you and repeat throughout the day as a way of focusing on the lesson.

The daily actions and mantras will help you bring your Warrior Goddess practice into your busy daily life, because they are simple and easy to do even while you're juggling work and social calendars. This way, you'll take a bit of Warrior Goddess Training with you into each day, and the journey will open up and strengthen new pathways and habits that will let you continue developing your own way of living in Warrior Goddess Wisdom even after you've finished the book.

No matter how you choose to use *Warrior Goddess Wisdom*, I hope you will always remember that the wisdom you seek is inside you. May this book help you peel back the layers of everything that is not you to reveal the core essence of your radiant, powerful, and sweet Warrior Goddess self.

The thing that is really hard, and really amazing, is giving up on being perfect and beginning the work of becoming yourself.
—Anna Quindlen

Many of us hold an image in our minds of who we think we should be, and we constantly compare ourselves to this imaginary version of ourselves. Anytime we fall short of this standard by not being pretty enough, successful enough, smart enough, or fill-in-the-blank enough, we judge ourselves harshly.

The truth of the matter is that we will always fall short of perfection when we compete against an imagined version of ourselves. You are perfectly imperfect, just as you are. Free yourself from the imaginary chains of perfection. You are the only one who can do so.

TODAY'S MANTRA

I am whole. I am powerful. I am divine. I am enough.

*One of the secrets to staying young is to always do
things you don't know how to do, to keep learning.*
—Ruth Reichl

Sometimes we stop ourselves from doing new things because we want to do it "right" right away. We're not willing to be messy or clumsy, or to make mistakes. But trying to always do things right can make us rigid, and never trying something new can keep us isolated in our old routines.

Imagine yourself looking at the world with a beginner's mind, and being willing to try new things. This means you are also willing to be messy, clumsy, and imperfect. That's what beginners do.

TODAY'S ACTION

Make a commitment to learn something new. Have you always wanted to knit, roller skate, skydive, or play an instrument? Try it! Be a beginner and see what calls to you.

Wrinkles should merely indicate where smiles have been.
—Mark Twain

My favorite thing about wrinkles (yes, you can have a favorite thing about wrinkles!) is that they can be a gauge for happiness. The more lines around my mouth, the more I've laughed; and the more crow's feet around my eyes, the more I've smiled. Despite what TV, magazines, and popular culture tell us, wrinkles are a natural, beautiful, normal part of our expressive faces. They are only flaws if we let them be, if that is our perspective. This is true of many physical flaws that we women are taught to buy into.

TODAY'S ACTION

Think of a few (two or three) of your physical "flaws" and write them down. If your wrinkles are a gauge of joy, what positives do your other "flaws" represent? For example, stretch marks might represent the birth of a beloved child or a new muscle. Next to each "flaw," write something positive that it represents. Notice how each one helps you gain a new perspective.

When you encounter difficulties and contradictions, do not try to break them, but bend them with gentleness and time.
—Saint Francis de Sales

Bravery is often equated with smashing through walls like a roaring bull, or leveling everything in your path like a foolhardy bulldozer. While this type of fierce push is occasionally needed, the equally potent forces of gentleness and patience are more effective at bending and melting something to your way—and they can be just as courageous.

Next time you find yourself in a conflict or disagreement that would normally upset or trigger you, try bringing your gentleness to the situation instead and see what happens.

TODAY'S MANTRA

I am like water. I flow continuously and overcome all obstacles with ease.

We are braver and wiser because they existed,
those strong women and strong men. . . We are
who we are because they were who they were.
—Maya Angelou

Teachers, friends, mentors, guides. Strangers, fellow goddesses, comic book superheroes, and movie heroines. Who are the women and men in your life who have inspired you? Who has helped make you strong and brave by their example? Every time we think about and enumerate the people who have inspired us, and remember the qualities they've modeled for us, those qualities become a more integral part of our way of being. The more we practice gratitude for those influences in our lives, the more their presence shines through in our actions.

TODAY'S ACTION

Take a few moments to sit in gratitude for every person who has ever inspired you. Imagine a riot of gratitude: glasses raised to toast to each other, happy high fives, and big bear hugs of love. Imagine holding a grand thank-you party for all the wise and courageous role models who are woven into the cloth of your being.

Life is too short for shoes that hurt your feet, friends that make you feel bad about yourself, and jobs that crush your soul. Take a chance. Make a change. The time is now.

—Lisa Lewtan

The time is now to buy a pair of shoes that fit your feet. Ones you can run and skip and dance in. Almost magically, once we begin to make changes in our lives, it's easier and easier to make more positive changes. If making a particular change seems overwhelming, then it's usually time to break it down. Baby steps in those comfortable new shoes can be the key to success.

For instance, if finding a new job seems too big, maybe reaching out to a college classmate who knows your field doesn't. While you most likely won't land a new job overnight, one thing does lead to another, and nothing happens without taking that first smallest step.

TODAY'S ACTION

Find one baby step toward your goal that you can work on comfortably without feeling overwhelmed. When you've completed this step, find the next one.

There is a fountain of youth: it is your mind, your talents, the creativity you bring to your life and the lives of people you love. When you learn to tap this source, you will truly have defeated age.
—Sophia Loren

Sometimes we forget about the importance of being creative, especially when "more important" things get in our way. We tend to push creativity aside if it's not making us money, or isn't helping our lives in some tangible way.

In reality, being creative just for creativity's sake enhances the mind, the body, and the spirit. Your fountain of youth *is* your creative approach to each and every day. Does this mean you have to be a prizewinning writer, have your paintings hang in a museum, or play at Carnegie Hall? Of course not. Creativity lies in the doing—not in the result.

TODAY'S ACTION

Do something creative today with no end goal in mind. Draw, write, paint, play an instrument, crochet, try a new recipe—whatever it is that makes your creative spirit feel alive. Notice how it feels to do this thing, with no result in mind.

How do I become still?
By flowing with the stream.
—Lao Tzu

One aspect of stillness is the absence of our relentless inner critic whose opinions, judgments, and complaints throw us off track. If we spend a lot of time listening to that noise, we become entangled in frustration, worry, and comparison, all of which put us at odds with the natural flow of life. And what happens when we flow with the stream? We accept each moment as it is. We quiet our inner nag. We give up the "shoulds," the "if onlys," and the "have tos." We live in the moment and go where the day takes us.

TODAY'S MANTRA

Notice the mind's tendency to judge, complain, or opine. And when it does, say, "Hello, new day! Today I choose to flow with the stream and listen from my heart for what my next step is."

The beginning is the most important part of the work.
—Plato

Nothing changes, evolves, grows, or moves forward without a beginning—and for this reason the beginning can be the hardest step of any journey. Beginnings are this wonderful mix of idealized outcomes and uncertainty (and maybe anxiety) about how we will get there. But of course the only way we will know if we can make our idea a reality is to take the journey.

It doesn't matter if the beginning is rocky, or if you don't feel a hundred percent confident in where you are going; what matters is that you *begin*—and that you keep beginning over and over again.

TODAY'S ACTION

In your mind, work backward from your goal until you have a task that will aim you in the right direction, but is so simple that your heart leaps at the chance to do it. Remember, you can't ever really accomplish a goal— only a *series of actions* toward that goal.

Now that I knew fear, I also knew it was not permanent. As powerful as it was, its grip on me would loosen. It would pass.
—Louise Erdrich

It's tempting to think that the fears you are experiencing today are permanent residents of your psyche; that your worries and anxieties will haunt you forever like ghosts. But no matter how fierce or large your fears may be, they are all temporary visitors, and they show up to teach us something about ourselves.

Our job is twofold: to figure out what our fears can teach us, and to let them go when the time comes. Sometimes we get so used to being afraid of someone or something in our lives that we don't notice those particular fears no longer serve a purpose, and we need to let them go. For instance, if I'm afraid I'll never be a success, but I have a good job that I love, maybe it's time to tell the failure monster goodbye.

TODAY'S ACTION

Name a fear you are currently carrying and imagine it is a temporary visitor that you can sit down and have a cup of tea with. What will you learn from that fear before it goes on its way?

*At the center of your being you have the answer; you know
who you are and you know what you want.*

—Lao Tzu

When we look outside into the world, we find myriad ideas about who we are "supposed" to be and what we "should" want in our lives. Everything from advertising to the opinions of friends and family informs who we think we should be. While many of these ideas may be well intentioned, the truth is that you are the only one who knows what you really want and what is best for you.

The Warrior Goddess path is about cultivating the relationship with yourself, and this means learning how to tap into the power of your intuition. Intuition makes its appearance only when you get still, go inside, and focus with your heart on what you want and need. If you listen, intuition will speak to you about small daily issues and your bigger problems and opportunities as well.

TODAY'S MANTRA

Take a moment to get still and silent. Go inside and focus on what you really want in your life. After a few moments, say the following: "I trust my inner knowing, I listen to my deepest wisdom, and I will not lead myself astray."

The secret of genius is to carry the spirit of the child into old age, which means never losing your enthusiasm.
—Aldous Huxley

I n my book *Awaken Your Inner Fire*, I write about the importance of cultivating what I call elder mind and child mind. The elder mind is the wisdom of the elders of the tribe, the learned counselor and advisor. Child mind reflects the excitement, exuberance, and curiosity of a little one. The balance between elder mind and child mind is such a special space to be in, because it allows for both the wisdom of old age and the enthusiasm of childhood. When we approach our life with these two attributes in mind, surprising things can happen.

TODAY'S ACTION

Name a situation that you need to bring your elder mind and child mind to. What is your inner wisdom telling you? What could your enthusiastic child tell you about that same situation? I invite you to notice these two aspects of yourself, and to call on them when needed. I bet you'll think of a solution you've never seen before. Genius!

Never tell a young person that anything cannot be done. God may have been waiting centuries for someone ignorant enough of the impossible to do that very thing.
—G. M. Trevelyan

It is theoretically impossible to touch hot coals and not get burned. Yet, as a certified firewalk instructor, I have led thousands of people over burning hot coals. When someone first walks on coals, the belief that "fire always burns" disappears before their very eyes. And suddenly the world is full of new possibilities.

This is the gift and lesson of firewalking, and it is analogous to our lives. If we can walk on fire, what other seemingly impossible things can we do? Or, looked at another way, what else do you believe about yourself and your abilities that isn't true? There is plenty of "that can't be done" negativity in the world, but change happens when we stand firm in the wild realms of the impossible, improbable, and miraculous. We are far more powerful than we realize.

TODAY'S ACTION

Take ten minutes to list as many things as you can that you've accomplished despite once thinking them "impossible." Keep this list to inspire you to achieve the impossible with the challenges you face in your life now.

You are much more than just a businesswoman or
a mom or a student. You are a divine, irreplaceable,
one-of-a-kind, amazing, loving, eternal being, and
your value comes from that fact alone.
—Kimberly Giles

While you likely play many different roles in your life, be careful not to confuse what you do with who you are. The roles we play will change over time, and clinging to them or demanding others reciprocate only leads to suffering. When we use up energy trying to fulfill a role that we're no longer needed for or called to, we inevitably feel less like our divine, irreplaceable self and more like a confused, overwhelmed victim.

Remember, when one role ends, another begins—and you get to choose how to play it. But no matter how much you love, like, or dislike playing a particular role, it won't come close to defining the totality of your being, the Magnificence of Life that you are.

TODAY'S MANTRA

Today I will release or change a role that no longer serves me. I will remember that who I am is far greater than any role I play.

I did not want my tombstone to read,
"She kept a really clean house."
—Ann Richards

There's nothing I love more than adventure. And the good news is that you don't have to be a swashbuckling pirate queen or a battle babe in shiny armor to find it—because adventure is all around you. The goal is to see the adventure (or, better yet, create it) in everyday moments.

Kids are especially good at this, so if you have kids, ask them to help you envision an adventure while you run errands or cook dinner. It's amazing what their imaginations can come up with. Adventures don't have to be big, either—it could be as simple as taking a car ride down an unfamiliar street, trying a new restaurant, or taking a painting class. The main thing about these adventures is that they nourish you, which ultimately helps you figure out what's important to you. What do you want it to say on your tombstone?

TODAY'S ACTION

What's something you can do to create adventure in your daily life? Start a list of small adventures you want to take. Put this list in a place where you'll see it and make sure to treat yourself to at least one adventure a week.

As human beings, our greatness lies not so much in being able to remake the world as in being able to remake ourselves.
—Mahatma Gandhi

In my view, the world is simply a reflection of those who live in it. When you change your internal perceptions, and how you see the world, your external world changes as well—and the universe feeds more of the same to you. So if you were to practice moving from anger to action, or from a place of complaining about what you don't have to being grateful for what you do, you would likely feel less anger, be more active, and become even more grateful for more blessings. And the more love, joy, and peace you see in the world, the more you will attract those attributes in the future. As we remake ourselves in this way, not only do we see the world as a better place, but the world also becomes a better place.

TODAY'S MANTRA

I invite love, harmony, and joy into my life and trust the Universe to provide me with my greatest good.

*You won't forget a woman like her. Once you cross
paths with Magic it's hard to see life the same.*
—Nikki Rowe

In our modern society, believing in "magic" is often portrayed as childish, foolish, or even crazy. But the truth is that magic is inside us and all around us. I know this because I feel it and see it.

There is a great wonder and mystery to our very existence. When we adjust our perspective, we see that everything that occurs becomes magical and the world becomes a much brighter place. A child's smile is magic. A tree in full bloom is magic. A deer grazing by the side of the road is magic. Magic abounds if we know where to look. The truth is that we all have magic inside of us, and this includes you. It's time to get in touch with yours.

TODAY'S ACTION

What makes you feel magical? Is it decorating an altar with fresh flowers and a beautiful scarf? Spending an evening dining by candlelight? Walking barefoot and reconnecting with the earth? Today, do something to bring you in touch with your divine magic.

Every truth has two sides; it is well to look at both,
before we commit ourselves to either.

—Aesop

Human beings are natural-born storytellers. We're telling ourselves tales all the time. And almost all of them involve things like right or wrong, good or bad, truth or untruth. But in the vast majority of cases, stories are open to interpretation.

The stories we tell ourselves are based on the truth *as we see it*, which doesn't mean someone else can't see things differently. When we remember this, we can explore all the different angles and perspectives of any story, and see how what is true for us may not be true for someone else. From this place of understanding we can hold our truth with love and compassion without needing to make another wrong.

TODAY'S ACTION

Today, be with your truth and let others be with theirs. To do this, let go of the need to be right, argue your point, or have the last word. Simply let others hold their truth, and hold yours in your heart as well.

Nothing in life is to be feared, it is only to be understood. Now is the time to understand more, so that we may fear less.

—Marie Curie

Curiosity is the antidote to fear. We only fear what we don't know or haven't accomplished yet because we think we *should* know it, or know how to get where we want to be. Fear may be a constant, but the desire to understand easily outweighs it in almost any situation. The first woman to win the Nobel Prize certainly knew this. Consider the difference between saying "I can't change careers" and the more curious approach, "What's the likelihood that I could change careers in the next year?" In order to evaluate this question, you need to deepen your understanding of all the factors at play in that idea. The understanding will lead to less fear, and more action. Now is the time.

TODAY'S ACTION

Think of a big personal fear related to how you operate in your relationships or commitments in the world. Ask yourself a question about the chance of your most desired outcome happening. What do you need to get curious about?

What you do makes a difference, and you have to
decide what kind of difference you want to make.
—Jane Goodall

Intent is the crux of every action we take. While you
can't predict the outcome of any given situation or
even the effect your action may or may not have on it,
you can be completely aware of your intent and focus.

With this in mind, you can ask yourself in any situation, what is my intent behind this action I'm about
to take? Is it coming from a place of love or fear? Do
I want to create peace or cause drama? Consider what
kind of difference you want to make in the world.

TODAY'S MANTRA

Let every action I take today carry the intent of love
rather than fear.

Peace is accepting today, releasing yesterday,
and giving up the need to control tomorrow.
—Lori Deschene

If we try to control our surroundings, or look ahead and plan for every possible outcome in a situation, we waste precious energy in an effort of futility. Instead of trying to control people, places, or things, or account for the potential outcome in a situation, take a breath and relax into the feeling of uncertainty.

What's going to happen next is uncertain, whether or not we think we're in control. If we think we're in control, we set ourselves up for pain and drama. But if we let go and surrender to the fact that we aren't in control, and that's okay, we can find peace in whatever comes our way. There's nothing to fear about not being in control; it's just another belief to let go of.

TODAY'S MANTRA

I do not control life. I do not know what will come next. I am at peace with the unknown.

She wasn't looking for a knight.
She was looking for a sword.
—Atticus Poetry

As young girls, many of us are taught to believe that we are princesses in need of saving or damsels in distress looking for knights to come to our rescue. While there's nothing wrong with being a princess, or even looking for a knight, the Warrior Goddess path is about recognizing that both of these energies are already inside of you right now. There's no need to look for a knight or a savior, because *you* are the one you've been waiting for. You have both goddess and warrior energy within whenever the situation requires it.

TODAY'S ACTION

Practice harnessing your warrior goddess energy. First, make a goddess gesture—maybe it's a curtsy, a wave, or a generous hug to the universe. Then make a gesture that embodies warrior energy—flex your muscles, karate kick, or stand at attention. Now combine these two movements to discover a gesture that evokes a balance of your unique warrior goddess energy. Call on this energy by remembering or reenacting this movement when needed.

Oh, I'm full of fear. I care about things; therefore, I have fears.
I like to think I'm brave, which is different. Brave means you're
able to admit that you care. If you care, you are vulnerable.
—Claire Danes

Being brave isn't about being hard and impenetrable. True bravery rests in our willingness to be vulnerable and tender, and to show up in spite of our fears. Whenever your inner judge tells you, "I must be brave and push through—I have to deny my feelings and stay strong," challenge yourself to flip the script. Try this instead: "I embrace bravery by telling the truth, by honoring my fears but not letting them steer the ship, and by showing up fully in my mind, heart and body. I know that this might hurt, because I care deeply. I am brave as I take the risk of sharing what I usually hide with those I love. I am here for this." Boom. Bravery.

TODAY'S MANTRA

I am brave in my honesty. I am brave in my fears. I am brave in my vulnerability. I am brave.

Renew, release, let go. Yesterday's gone. There's nothing you can do to bring it back. You can't "should've" done something. You can only DO something. Renew yourself. Release that attachment. Today is a new day!

—Steve Maraboli

If I had to pick the one thing that most depletes personal energy and wastes time on a massive scale, it would be regret.

Let's make a pact to offer up all of our "should haves," "should not haves," and "if onlys," and release any regrets we are clinging to for that which has gone before. Let's commit to bringing the gentle, compassionate energy of our inner goddess and fierce determination of our inner warrior to our activities of this day.

TODAY'S ACTION

Think of a particular "should have" or "if only" regret that you've been clinging to and write it down on a scrap of paper. Ball it up. Throw it away. Even burn it in a safe place as a ritual. It's done and over. There's no need to hold on to it anymore.

When the whole world is silent,
even one voice becomes powerful.
—Malala Yousafzai

Sometimes we find ourselves in a place where our viewpoint is in the minority, or perhaps we are even all alone in our opinion. That doesn't mean your voice and your experiences are not important. In fact, when others are silent, your voice can be the one that brings change, healing, and clarity. Your experience, your beliefs, your truth may be shared by others who are afraid to speak up.

TODAY'S MANTRA

My voice is the voice of thousands unspoken.

The whole universe is friendly to us and conspires only
to give the best to those who dream and work.
—A. P. J. Abdul Kalam

On days when things don't go as we had hoped or planned, it's tempting to believe that the whole world, or even the whole universe, is out to get us. In these moments it's important to look around and notice how the world really is.

For instance, a tree provides shade that you have the benefit of sheltering in. A bird sings a song that you get to hear. The ground beneath your feet supports your every step. Neighbors and friends show their love and compassion by sharing their company, and perhaps a meal. When you look closer, you can see a multitude of ways that prove the world is a friendly place, if you remain open to receiving the friendship and compassion that are at work all around us.

TODAY'S ACTION

Notice all the acts of kindness, compassion, and support that you see today for yourself and others. Nothing is too small—they are all messages of love simply waiting for you to receive them—and pass them on.

When someone shows you who they are,
believe them the first time.

—Maya Angelou

So often we want to see things in people that aren't really there, or we hold on to our idea of who someone is rather than seeing who they actually are. If a person betrays your trust, it's okay to forgive them. But it's also okay to create a boundary. In my view, there are no bad people in the world, but there are people who take actions that aren't in alignment with what I want in my life today. We're all on our own path, and I have the right to choose who I want in mine.

When you don't see the people around you for who they are, but rather what you want them to be, you won't be able to have a relationship built on truth. Letting go of the ideas you have created and seeing others as they are does mean you might have to let go of the person. It might mean you simply start over, seeing and accepting them for who they are, not who you want them to be.

TODAY'S MANTRA

May I see others as they are, not as I wish them to be.

For beautiful eyes, look for the good in others;
for beautiful lips, speak only words of kindness.
—Audrey Hepburn

Some days it's not all that easy to see the good in others. When we look at the woman with the crying baby in the grocery store, we might think of how much of an interruption that is. We might judge her for bringing a tired baby to the store, not thinking how she might not have anyone to help her at home.

On a better day, we might see the loving, caring, exhausted mother she is. We might look her in the eye and see beauty. We might speak to her kindly, and suddenly the world is a little bit better. The same could go for you, too. When you look yourself in the eye, do you see your own good? When you speak to yourself, do you do so with kind words?

TODAY'S MANTRA

May I see with beautiful eyes and speak with kind lips.

They keep saying that beautiful is something a girl needs
to be. But honestly? Forget that. Don't be beautiful. Be
angry, be intelligent, be witty, be klutzy, be interesting, be
funny, be adventurous, be crazy, be talented—there are
an eternity of other things to be other than beautiful.
—Nikita Gill

Society tells us what beautiful is, but no woman on this planet meets those expectations. (And we all know that even images of supermodels are altered prior to publication!) While looking good can certainly make you feel good, the moment you put your idea of beauty above all the other wonderful things that you are, comparison and self-judgment are sure to follow. In what ways are you fascinating? Wild? Inspired? These are the things that make you bold and beautiful, inside and out.

TODAY'S ACTION

When you find yourself fixating on your appearance, lovingly bring yourself back to the internal qualities you enjoy about yourself beyond your physicality. Then, take a gratitude inventory inside and out: strong thighs to take you where you want to go; a mouth to express yourself and taste nourishing foods; a courageous heart open to new experiences.

The question is not what you look at, but what you see.
—Henry David Thoreau

Beauty is always around us, but we don't always see it—especially if we choose not to see it. On gloomy days or when we're in a funk, we may unknowingly turn a blind eye to beauty, or to kindnesses, because it doesn't fit with what we want to feel. Sadness and grief are normal human emotions, but we want to be able to recognize the difference between emoting and wallowing.

One test for this is to think of something that you normally find beautiful and see how you react to it. If you feel yourself saying something like, "Ugh, that's not even pretty," you may be wallowing. On the other hand, if you say, "This is beautiful, but I'm sad," you are likely emoting. Paying attention to your attitude and reactions can keep you from getting trapped in wallowing, even when you hit a rough emotional patch.

TODAY'S ACTION

See where you resist beauty or positivity. Ask yourself why you're feeling that way. Notice, don't judge, if you're wallowing. Allow yourself to feel.

We're all under the same sky and walk the same earth;
we're alive together during the same moment.
—Maxine Hong Kingston

When astronauts first viewed the earth from space and witnessed this incredible blue planet we live on, all borders and boundaries became insignificant. No matter our country or culture or lifestyle, we all share this small planet and this human experience. All of us yearn for love, acceptance, and purpose. All of us have tasted grief and sadness.

Imagine a world in which we all acknowledge that we're human beings. Imagine a world in which we resolve to treat each other equally no matter our skin color, religion, age, sexual preference or orientation, nationality, or political views. In point of fact, we're all more alike than we are different, and once we begin to realize that, we can begin to find our common ground and resolve our differences, big and small.

TODAY'S ACTION

Take a moment to marvel at the wonder of being alive and living under the same sky with your fellow humans. When you see others today, remember that you are seeing yourself.

I've always loved butterflies because they remind us
that it's never too late to transform ourselves.
—Drew Barrymore

One of the biggest lies we tell ourselves is that we're "too old" to do something, or that it's "too late," or that our best days are behind us. The truth is that it's never too late to transform yourself and your life. In fact, transformation can only begin now, not in the past or the future.

Here's another little secret about transformation: It's not a one-time event. It's a continuous process. And it doesn't happen all at once. Even the caterpillar spends between two weeks and a year in the cocoon (depending on the species). So take your time, but recognize that you can and will continue to transform.

TODAY'S ACTION

Where is one place in your life where you feel yourself budding out or ready to start a transformation? Spend a few days cocooning this idea by writing about what that change will look like. Describe where you want to go, and then start the process by taking small action steps toward your transformation.

What a lovely surprise to finally discover
how unlonely being alone can be.
—Ellen Burstyn

One of the biggest benefits of doing inner work to really get to know and love yourself is that you are no longer afraid to be alone. That's because when we love and accept ourselves for who we are, we immediately become our own best friend, someone we're interested in spending more time with and getting to know better. And we become our own biggest supporter, knowing how smart, interesting, funny, and fun we are. Great peace and great opportunity can be found in solitude. You get to decide what you want to do, you can check in on yourself, and you can enjoy your own company.

TODAY'S ACTION

Find a moment of solitude (even if it takes hiding from the kids in the bathroom for a few minutes). Use it to say hello to yourself, see how you're really doing, and catch up on how you've been treating yourself recently. If you find that you haven't been treating yourself as nicely as you would your best friend, take this moment of solitude to recommit to loving and supporting yourself through thick and thin.

If opportunity doesn't knock, build a door.
—Milton Berle

We all have things we want to do, goals we want to accomplish. Like it or not, challenges and obstacles will arise as we pursue these things. When this happens, we can wait around for someone to knock on our door (literally or figuratively) to solve our problem or remove our obstacles. Or we can remember the innate power we all have that allows us to find creative solutions to any problems we encounter. Look at a problem in a different way. As the old saying goes, if we continue to do what we've always done, we'll get what we always get.

TODAY'S ACTION

When challenges arise today, make a mental list of creative ideas and solutions to overcome the issue. Part of our genius as humans can be found in our creativity; remember to cultivate yours when it comes to problem-solving.

Don't wait for someone to bring you flowers.
Plant your own garden and decorate your own soul.
—Mario Quintana

When we spend time waiting for someone else to make us happy—whether that be small things like bringing us presents or doing the dishes or the larger things like loving us how we want them to—we are giving away our power. It's good to be straightforward and ask people for things that you want from them. Otherwise how can we expect them to know?

The real trick is to also know what we need to ask from ourselves. Are the dishes in the sink bothering you? Clean them. Do you want flowers? Buy them. You are your own partner, first and foremost, whether you currently have a beloved or not. Today, ask, how can you live in harmonious partnership with yourself?

TODAY'S ACTION

Is there something you've been waiting for someone else to do or give you? Give yourself this gift today.

I am constantly amazed by Tina Fey.
And I am Tina Fey.
—Tina Fey

As children, many of us were taught to be quiet, to be small, to be seen and not heard. As a result, some of us have the idea that by taking pride in our abilities or saying something nice about ourselves— even to ourselves—is a sign that we are conceited or vain, or are being a braggart. But there is absolutely nothing wrong with feeling proud of your accomplishments and voicing it.

Undoing the habit of playing small can take some conscious effort. The truth is that *you are amazing.* Yes, I'm talking about you! Every single human on this planet is a unique creation of the Divine, and it's time to claim your amazing grace.

TODAY'S MANTRA

I am constantly amazed by (your name). And I am (your name)!

We must dare to think "unthinkable" thoughts. We must learn to explore all the options and possibilities that confront us in a complex and rapidly changing world.
—J. William Fulbright

The moment we think we know everything about anything, we close our minds to possibility. Learning, growing, and creating occur when we become open to thinking in new ways, examining new ideas, and, most importantly, admitting that we do not have all the answers. When we bring our minds to the edge of the unknown, we create the possibility that the unthinkable and the unimaginable can enter into our reality. There is great mystery all around us; and when we listen to that mystery, new options and possibilities start to flourish.

TODAY'S ACTION

Sit in meditation today and allow your mind to rest and be silent. Settle into the unknown and receive answers from the mystery around you.

If you wish to heal your sadness or anger,
seek to heal the sadness or anger of others.
—Ana Castillo

Sometimes we can get so caught up in our own lives and our own issues that we forget the importance of helping others. The irony is that anytime we help others, we also help ourselves. This is because doing so takes us out of our own problems and reminds us that we are all in this beautiful life together.

Helping others does not mean you must take grandiose actions, or even any action at all. Oftentimes just a few words like "I understand," "I see you," and "I'm listening" act like a healing balm on tender wounds. Be mindful of the opportunity to be helpful to someone today, even if that is only to listen and let them know you care. Rather than try to fix others, walk beside them, acknowledge them, and share the love that is in your heart.

TODAY'S MANTRA

May my gentle presence soothe wounds.

The best thing you could do is master the chaos in you.
You are not thrown into the fire, you are the fire.
—Mama Indigo

I used to hate chaos, because it meant that no matter how carefully I had planned things, they'd gone completely haywire. What I've come to find now, though, is that chaos is the universe's way of reminding me that I am not in control. When you embrace chaos as it arises, you are learning how to surf the waves of life rather than getting swamped by them. That is what mastering the chaos is about.

Chaos teaches us to let go in ways that few things can. When we take the spirit of surrender into chaos, we are bringing the fire of transformation from our very being into the world. When we loosen our grip on our plans, we open ourselves up to the best possible outcome.

TODAY'S ACTION

One way to find out what you're trying to control is by doing a body scan. While thinking about things going on in your life right now, notice if you start clenching your jaw, tensing your shoulders, or fidgeting in your chair. When you notice tension, stop and face the situation. Rather than trying to control it, bring the spirit of surrender to your body, and the situation. Breathe and let go.

You can get help from teachers, but you are going to have to
learn a lot by yourself, sitting alone in a room.

—Dr. Seuss

Teachers are fabulous, blessed beings who can help to guide us toward where we want and need to be. They can remind us to stay on track, supporting and nourishing us along the way. They can tell us new stories and teach us new skills. The purpose of every teacher you meet on your path is to bring you to the greatest teacher of all: the one inside of you. All the wisdom that you could ever desire lies deep within yourself. The best teachers are the ones who help you find what you already knew all along.

TODAY'S ACTION

Spend a few minutes in silent meditation (or longer if you can), as this is one of the best ways to get in touch with the teacher within.

*It wasn't books that inspired me to write. For me inspiration
was simple, immediate: I got it from eating, dancing, talking.
I got it from life lived, things touched, from sensuality, from
love of life, from our irrefutable connection to the earth.*

—Laura Esquivel

Everything in your life can be an adventure and an inspiration the moment you see it that way. That bite of nourishing food. That joke shared with a friend or a stranger. The cool metal of the door handle. Your body as an extension of the earth beneath your feet. Let your senses roam free, and keep exploring the sights, sounds, and smells all around you. Both the world around you and within you are a beautiful mystery waiting for you to delve in deeply.

TODAY'S MANTRA

Inspiration is all around me. I only need eyes to see it, skin to touch it, ears to hear it, and a heart open to feeling it.

Love yourself so much that when someone
treats you wrong, you recognize it.

—Rena Rose

I f you're a parent and someone treats your child badly in school or on the playground, you recognize it immediately. And you most likely speak up for your child. Ditto if you're a teacher and one student is dominating the discussion. Or if someone insults your best friend at a party, you stick up for her. You love your children or your students or your friends, and you want to see no harm come to them.

So the question is, how much do you love yourself? Are you willing to speak up for yourself over small wrongs, such as being cut off in the grocery store line, or bigger ones, like when someone utters an ethnic slur that offends you? If you're in an abusive relationship, do you feel as though you deserve to be treated that way? Or do you acknowledge it and remove yourself from situations where others are not treating you with the respect you deserve? When we love ourselves, we treat ourselves in a loving and kind way, just as we treat the others in our lives.

DAILY MANTRA

I love myself. I will stand up for myself. I will ask to be treated with respect.

I do not want to be the angel of any home; I want for myself what I want for other women—absolute equality. After that is secured then men and women can take turns being angels.
—Agnes Macphail

Angel. Mother. Daughter. Sister. Caretaker. Princess. These are some roles that have traditionally been assigned to women, but these roles are not you. Remember: you can stop playing a part anytime you feel it no longer serves you. And you can fulfill your emotional desires and commitments to yourself and others without strict adherence to any one role. You can love your parents without being their idea of a perfect daughter. You can be vulnerable and need help without being a princess trapped in a tower.

TODAY'S ACTION

If you want to change your roles, make a list of them. Next to each role, write down which parts you enjoy playing and which you don't. Armed with your list, negotiate with the others in your life. Start applying your "no" to the parts you do not enjoy, and your conscious "yes" to the parts you do. You get to create your roles and what they mean to you.

Choose to focus your time, energy, and conversation around
people who inspire you, support you, and help you to grow
you into your happiest, strongest, wisest self.
—Karen Salmansohn

One of the things I love about Buddhism is the importance it places on sangha, a community of practitioners, as a tool for progress on the spiritual path and living a fulfilled life. It's important to continue to gather and maintain this group of fellow travelers.

Think of the people in your life who inspire and support you. Be sure to include the ones who challenge you to be the best you possible, and who invite you to grow in the way that you know your heart wants. Now think of how much time you have spent with these people in the last month, either in person or in conversation if they aren't physically close by. How does your contact with them compare to how you'd like it to be?

TODAY'S ACTION

Who is in your sangha? Reach out to at least one of the people who challenges and supports you. Email, call, text, write a love note—whatever it takes to get that communication flowing.

Within every woman there is a wild and natural creature, a powerful force, filled with good instincts, passionate creativity, and ageless knowing. Her name is Wild Woman, but she is an endangered species.
—Clarissa Pinkola Estés

Think back to a time when you were wild. When you embraced a physical or emotional challenge that took everything within you. When you were attuned to yourself and your environment in a cycle of courageous call and response. Most likely, this was a time you allowed yourself to put down your armor and pick up the tools of passionate and untamed creativity. When we reconnect to our Wild Woman, we learn things about ourselves. We kick ass at our chosen tasks, and we flow along our chosen path with grace and strength.

TODAY'S ACTION

Take some time to do something wild! Move energy with your voice, beat a drum, play with bright-color paint, or dance with your whole body. Unleash the uninhibited woman within today!

Letting go doesn't mean you stop caring.
It means you stop trying to force others to.
—Mandy Hale

How do I make my partner love me? How do I get my boss to value me? How do I make my kids appreciate me?

What do all these questions have in common? They ask how we can change other people. And the truth is that we can't. What we *can* do is let go of our need for approval, our need for love, our desire to make others act in a way we predetermine.

We are not responsible for others' thoughts or actions. While it's perfectly appropriate to want to be appreciated, you don't have to be upset that your boss doesn't value you. You don't even have to be upset that your partner doesn't love you, as radical as that sounds. Once you let go of expectations, you can either stay or leave, but you have dropped the weight of demanding that things be any way other than how they are.

TODAY'S MANTRA

I'm letting go of my need for approval. I'm letting go of my expectations to change others.

It took me quite a long time to develop a voice,
and now that I have it, I am not going to be silent.
—Madeleine Albright

When you silence or temper your voice out of fear of not being heard, or accepted, or loved, you give away your power. And then it's no longer the outside world that is silencing you, but how you silence yourself that becomes the enemy.

It can take years for us to find our voice and the confidence to use it. This may be an ongoing internal battle. People may not listen to you. And that's okay! The important thing is to speak up from your unique and powerful voice, again and again, until it becomes second nature.

TODAY'S ACTION

Where have you been silencing your voice? Is there something you need to speak up for today? Make a list of things you want to speak up for in the near future.

I am not free while any woman is unfree, even
when her shackles are very different from my own.
—Audre Lorde

We are each responsible for doing what we can to secure our own freedom—to live the life we're meant to live. And we're also connected to all other women, no matter how much we may think we don't have things in common with them, no matter how different their lives may seem from our own.

We are all in this together. Instead of dragging each other down through comparison and competition, let's hand out keys and help unlock the old, burdensome chains that weigh us down.

TODAY'S ACTION

Watch for the habit to judge, compete, and compare with another one of your sisters today. Share a book, share your experiences and learnings, share your heart.

*My darling girl, when are you going to realize
that being normal is not necessarily a virtue?
It rather denotes a lack of courage.*
—Alice Hoffman

In my view there's no such thing as normal. "Normal" is just a mask that almost every person in the world wears at one time or another so as to not be noticed, not stick out from the crowd, not be judged, not risk doing big things. Being "normal" isn't who you are, and it isn't what you should strive to be.

If you were to live courageously from your inner passion, what might happen? You might anger some of your friends and family. They might say you're not acting like your "normal" self. And you might discover or rediscover your passion and purpose in life. So what if that passion isn't "normal"? Normal is not a virtue, and if normal means being the same as everyone else, well, no one is.

TODAY'S MANTRA

Today I will be my courageous self. Today I will live my courageous purpose. Today I will live from my courageous fire.

And those who were seen dancing were thought to
be insane by those who could not hear the music.
—Friedrich Nietzsche

You are on the path you are on for a reason. There will be those who don't understand your path, and those who refuse to even try to understand. Your job is to love those who don't understand you without judging them. This can be especially hard when they are judging you.

Be open to sharing your music with others without trying to convince them of anything. Tell them about what you're doing and why you're doing it. Tell them your calling. Invite them to talk about their paths as well. Show them that you don't judge them. And perhaps there will come a time when they don't judge you.

TODAY'S MANTRA

I will listen to the beat of my own drum and follow it today. I am making my own path.

It is the mark of an educated mind to be able
to entertain a thought without accepting it.
—Aristotle

It's so easy to attach to things that we hear or see—especially if they cause fear or anxiety in us. This is why it's so important to be able to step back and separate yourself from the influx of information that comes at you all the time. When we step back, we can take time to decide if the information or idea is actually true for us. Is it something that we consciously choose to accept? Or do we reject it? It's okay to choose either way. The point is that you have a choice. So stop, think, consider, and then make your move. Reclaim your power over your mind, and over your world, by making conscious decisions regarding what information you choose to attach to and what you will leave for someone else.

TODAY'S ACTION

Think of an idea someone wants you to accept—it could be about politics or religion or how to spend the weekend. Consider it thoughtfully. How does it add to or subtract from your purposeful life? What does your intuition tell you is true? When we practice thoughtful consideration, it becomes second nature.

You may not control all the events that happen to you,
but you can decide not to be reduced by them.
—Maya Angelou

One thing is certain in this life: things won't always go as we plan or hope. Say you don't get the job you want, or your significant other wants to end the relationship and you want to stay together. What's your first go-to in these big setbacks or changes? Will you react with frustration, anger, hatred, fear, victimization, or doubt?

Your Warrior Goddess superpower is not about forcing the world to conform to your desires, but rather responding to the world with strength when it doesn't. Nobody says it's easy when your world is falling apart. But if you've been practicing responding with grace, resiliency, and creativity over smaller setbacks, you've been building up a bank account of power and you can find it in yourself to choose the high road. Your power is in your choice.

TODAY'S MANTRA

I choose to own my power in the face of challenges today, and respond appropriately instead of reacting uncontrollably.

*Love yourself so much to the point that your energy
and aura rejects anyone who doesn't know your worth.*
—Billy Chapata

One place our inner voice, aka intuition, will speak to us using the language of silence is when we interact with other people. Notice how you feel around people when they come into your physical space. Do you feel brighter, perkier, and interested? Or does your inner light feel dimmed? Do you feel a sense of peace? Or do you feel bored, restless, or cautious? What is your intuition trying to tell you?

Sometimes the thinking mind will try to override these cues from our silent wisdom, saying things like, "It's okay, don't worry about that feeling . . ." But as our awareness matures, we learn to recognize and respect our intuitive feelings, to know that they are real, and to heed them. Choosing not to engage with people doesn't mean we are judging them; it means we are honoring our truth and respecting that their path is different from our own.

TODAY'S MANTRA

I am moving away from people who are not meant for me.

Happiness is self-generated as the mind becomes
still. As we become involved with the desires of the
world, we lose that centering, that stillness.
—Frederick Lenz

We've all experienced wanting, waiting, saving, hoping for some desired thing. We know that thing or person won't make our lives perfect—but we're pretty sure it will make us happy. It is so easy to be hooked by the desires of the world—a new car, a house, a job, even another human. Our desires aren't typically limited to external things, either, and oftentimes include recognition or success.

But lasting happiness doesn't come from grasping for objects or popularity. It comes from turning within and recognizing the still, joyful nature of your very being-ness. It arises from being comfortable in your own skin.

TODAY'S ACTION

Explore your inner happiness by creating space for your mind to rest into stillness. Breathe in and out. Let your thoughts go. Return to stillness over and over again, and you'll find your happy meter goes up naturally.

Owning our story can be hard but not nearly
as difficult as spending our lives running from it.
—Brené Brown

It is no easy task to fully embrace our complicated histories, including things we might have done or said that we regret or feel ashamed about. It takes effort, honesty, and bravery, but when you fully own the events from your past, they lose their power over you. The first step is realizing that you are the writer of your story, not a character in it. As the author, you can rewrite and recontextualize past events so that you're describing one fraction of your story—not the defining moment of it. For example, instead of saying "I am a failure," you could say "Things didn't work out as I planned, but then I . . ." Eventually, you will be able to talk about those painful past moments freely, and appreciate that they were necessary to make you who you are today.

TODAY'S ACTION

Think of a memory that stirs a twinge of regret, and write the story in your own words. Then go back and edit this story—not as a character, but as the author of your fate.

Diets, like clothes, should be tailored to you.
—Joan Rivers

There is no such thing as one size fits all. Not for physical diets and exercise, not for clothes, and not for spiritual paths. No matter what change you are seeking or what obstacles you're struggling with, there is no one prescription that works for everyone. While it may seem easier if someone would just tell you what to do, which eating program to follow, etc., this just isn't how it works.

Because we are all unique, our paths will be unique as well. Rather than trying to follow a regimen that doesn't suit you, I encourage you to take bits and pieces from everything and anything that inspires you to achieve your goals—be they physical, mental, emotional, or spiritual. Adapt them and learn to use your own inner wisdom, your own talents and traits, to develop a plan tailored exactly to you.

TODAY'S ACTION

Make up your own action today. What exercise or mantra would best serve you today? Use this chance to expand your creativity, get in touch with your needs, and implement your ideas. You've got this!

Anyone can slay a dragon ... but try waking up
every morning and loving the world all over again.
That's what takes a real hero.
—Brian Andreas

In the old-fashioned mythic story of the hero, a lone man ventures out to find his fortune, combat evil, save a woman or two, and demonstrate his strength against all obstacles.

In the modern story of the heroine Warrior Goddess, a lone woman ventures out to find herself, combat fear and doubt, reclaim her power and vibrancy, and demonstrate her strength of compassion and fierce love.

Waking up every morning and trying again to love the world *as you find it* is what makes you a powerful heroine. Remember, it's not just the dragons outside of you that need slaying (or, better yet, befriending) but the ones that are plaguing you internally.

TODAY'S MANTRA

I am the loving, kind heroine of my own story. I embrace my dragons, external and internal, and transform them through the power of love.

*The great thing about getting older is that
you don't lose all the other ages you've been.*
—Madeleine L'Engle

One thing I've noticed the older I get is how my spirit and my heart grow more with each day. I feel more comfortable in my own skin now than I ever did in my twenties. The movies and TV shows and mass media will tell you that you are supposed to go from awkward teen to confident young adult seemingly overnight. Then, before you know it, you are supposed to have to fight against the horrors of old age.

But that's just not the case. It takes time to ripen. Whether you consider yourself young or old or somewhere in between, it's never too early or late to start growing into your own skin. The older we get, the more memories, stories, and skills for becoming our best selves we accumulate. We know enough at forty not to jump headlong into a situation we got lost in at thirty. Whatever age you are now will help inform the age you are becoming. Remember, age is just a number, not an indication of how well your skin fits.

TODAY'S ACTION

Take a moment to be grateful for all the ways that you've ripened. Think of all the progress you've made in becoming the woman you are meant to be.

Don't look at your feet to see
if you are doing it right. Just dance.
—Anne Lamott

Insecurity is one of our biggest blocks to joy. If we don't try something new because we're worried about what other people are thinking, we're denying ourselves an opportunity to experience magic. This goes for dancing, eating new foods, traveling to exotic locales, taking classes—anything outside our usual routine. We're afraid of what might happen, that we might make a wrong move, or have to ask for help.

If you're having trouble breaking down your mental block in front of others, then start when you're alone. Enjoy doing something by yourself, without any inhibition, and then begin bringing your newfound joy, passion, and confidence with you as you do more new things with others.

TODAY'S ACTION

Put on your favorite song and close your eyes. Let your body play with the music. Let joy flow through you. Then ask yourself, "How can I bring this same feeling of freedom into my day?"

Nothing is impossible, the word itself says "I'm possible."
—Audrey Hepburn

I can vividly remember the times in my life when I heard something was "impossible." I heard it from family members, friends, and then myself. Because I believed what I was told without question, I agreed that it was impossible for me to pack up and move across the country, and I thought it was impossible that I would ever find my true calling. But once on the Warrior Goddess path, I began to entertain the thought, "This *is* possible . . ." The moment you let go of the belief that a thing is impossible, it becomes possible.

TODAY'S ACTION

What have you told yourself is impossible? Pick one thing—maybe it's homeownership, or skydiving, or breaking into your dream career. Now research a next possible step toward achieving the impossible. Check out some books on how to buy a house, or make a coffee date with someone who does your dream job. The more research you do, the easier it is to break down what action steps you need to make your impossible into "I'm possible."

I'm still learning to love the
parts of me that no one claps for.
—Rudy Francisco

Part of loving ourselves unconditionally means witnessing not just our unique inner beauty and strengths but also the parts of ourselves we don't like as much. Our bad habits, physical "flaws," and past mistakes are often the things we struggle to embrace. These are the parts we push into the shadows because we're afraid people will ridicule or dislike us because of them. We think they're not worthy of being seen, let alone celebrated.

These wounds need our self-love more than we know. It's not always easy, or pretty, and it may not get applause, but learning to love these shadow parts brings them into the light and allows us to love our entire being.

TODAY'S ACTION

Start a list of your shadow parts, the things about you that no one claps for. Each day, work on pouring loving-kindness into those cracks. Just a little every day can make a world of difference.

Life is a banquet, and most poor suckers are starving to death.
—Rosalind Russell

We've all experienced moments of indecision: Should I take that job? Should I move to this town? Should I commit to this person? Fear of failure can hold us back, and keep us from taking chances. It can starve us from the nourishment that a full life has to offer. If we don't take the job, move somewhere new, or go on that first date, we might save ourselves from being hurt, yes. But we will also lose out on the chance for joy, challenge, and gratification. Experience is a vital, wonderful teacher. After all, it's our "failures" that lead to a stockpile of wisdom.

TODAY'S ACTION

Have you been holding yourself back? Take some time to really think on this. You may find that you have a pattern of behaviors that all stem from the same fear. Once you identify what is holding you back, you can start to unravel it.

Love yourself first and everything else falls into line.
—Lucille Ball

The voice of your inner judge is not wise. Yes, it may be loud, persistent, and even authoritative at times. But it is not wise. That's because self-judgment comes from fear and causes closure.

Wisdom comes from self-love and self-acceptance, and it creates openings. When you catch yourself making a mistake and berating yourself, or you hear yourself replaying a mental story that says you are anything less than wonderful, that's your cue to bring love to yourself instead. Imagine yourself as a wise elder in those moments, one with a twinkle in her eye and infinite patience, humor, and equanimity. What would that wise elder say to her younger self? When we're in love, it seems a world of possibilities opens up to us. It can be the same when we love ourselves.

TODAY'S ACTION

Get still and comfy and silent and listen to what your loving self has to say to you. Maybe it's "go easy on yourself, sweetheart—everyone makes mistakes," or "there's a whole world of possibilities out there for you."

Someone I loved once gave me a box full of darkness.
It took me years to understand that this, too, was a gift.
—Mary Oliver, "The Uses of Sorrow"

When someone breaks a promise, betrays our trust, or abandons a commitment, it's natural to feel sorrow, grief, despair—even rage. But with time, these gifts of darkness can benefit us, because as we unpack the event, bring it to light and heal this hurt, we look deeper inside ourselves. We find things that made us capable of overcoming these obstacles—gifts that perhaps were in us all along, or that we developed as we healed. These gifts are all the sweeter for the bitterness from which they are born.

TODAY'S ACTION

List some gifts you have developed after going through difficulties with other people. What strengths have you found as you've moved through darkness? If you're still in the process, look at the gifts that are just seedlings, and ask how you can nurture them to grow fully and completely.

I learned that courage was not the
absence of fear, but the triumph over it.
—Nelson Mandela

This might sound strange, but I have become grateful for my fears. In fact, I've learned to love them. Fear is a guide, like a neon sign pointing at all the things we need to work on. When we experience fear, we know it's time to pay attention and find the source of the problem: What am I afraid of? What belief or idea do I need to heal so that I'm no longer afraid? What would happen if I didn't have this fear impeding my journey? If overcoming the fear isn't possible right now, just being aware of it and its source can help you take action in spite of feeling afraid. Really, your fears have your own best interests at heart—they want to keep you safe. So thank them for their concern, and then engage with what you fear from a place of empowerment and choice.

TODAY'S ACTION

Write down some of your fears, from minor anxieties to giant dreads. Can you see the sources? Write them down and bring a sense of conscious gratitude to your fears. They are pointing you in the right direction.

Ninety-nine percent of my worst days
never happened, except in my own mind.
—Mick Plaster

Many of us have adopted the idea that worrying is helpful; that somehow if we worry about things, we will be prepared for the worst. Instead of making us feel prepared for anything, though, worry destabilizes us. It chews on our self-confidence and sense of safety, and erodes our ability to respond with imagination and courage when things don't go according to plan.

The antidote to worry is faith, specifically faith that everything will work out fine, and even to our benefit. I have over fifty years of experience that everything has always worked out fine, and my gratitude for this fact expands my sense of faith.

TODAY'S ACTION

When you find yourself imagining the worst, take a moment to ground yourself in the truth of your experience. You are still here—everything has worked out fine in the end. You can count on yourself and imagine the best, and still get through tough times if they happen.

Angry people want you to see how powerful they are.
Loving people want you to see how powerful you are.
—Chief Red Eagle

If we turn on any news station, the negativity, pain, and power grabbing going on in the world can be overwhelming. I never ask people "what side" they support, because to me we are all on the same side: humanity. And it's up to us to love all of humanity—not just those who agree with us. If we find ourselves trapped in anger, needing to feel righteous or powerful over someone else and their beliefs, then we can be certain we have abandoned the all-important commitment to love each other. But when we spread love and support to all of our brothers and sisters, when we lift each other up, we change the world.

TODAY'S ACTION

Think of someone who digs in firmly on the other side of an issue about which you are passionate. Your mission now is to transform your frustration into loving-kindness and send it to them. Take a few moments to surround them with the intention of love and wanting what is best for them and all humanity.

Computers are useless. They can only give you answers.
—Pablo Picasso

What if there were no answers to some of life's biggest questions: Who are we? Why are we here? What is the meaning of all this?

At first glance, the idea that there are no answers can seem frightening, or even nihilistic, but that's not the intention here. Instead, notice which part of you asks those types of questions. Yep, you got it; it's the thinking mind. While the mind has many valuable and helpful qualities, "figuring it all out" isn't one of them. For this, we need to access the deep silent wisdom within each of us. When we look from within this place of wisdom at questions like these, we find that the answer is a beautiful mystery, and we can be at perfect peace with that.

TODAY'S ACTION

Put your book down and be silent for a moment. Take time to expand the energy of your heart, feeling it flow from your chest into the room around you, and then beyond—as far as it will take you. Feel connected to the vastness of the universal mysteries, and be at peace.

The more space there is in the relationship—
inner space—the more love there is because love
arises out of the inner spaciousness.
—Eckhart Tolle

Narrow channels of repetitive worries, controlling thoughts, and paralyzing fears lead us nowhere. What happens when you follow those pathways? You end up cornered in a dark, scary place.

From this point on, as soon as you feel a sense of confinement, stop. Recognize that you don't have to keep going down those channels. You can seek out a path of freedom. While you can't control your first thought about something, you can steer your mind to think of other things instead. You can open up space for more love.

TODAY'S ACTION

Today, when you start to notice your brain going down paths that don't lead to peace, take a big breath and stop. Tune in to the vast space within you and around you, and release into delicious freedom.

*I am looking forward enormously to getting back to the sea
again, where the overstimulated psyche can recover in the
presence of that infinite peace and spaciousness.*
—Carl Jung

When was the last time you went to the ocean, or wandered through a quiet forest? It's easy to forget that we are part of nature. We crave the touch and feel of water, earth, and living things. When we go for any stretch of time without access to the outdoors, the balance is tipped in our psyche—in favor of our thinking mind. Nature is one of the best healers of our overstimulated minds, and returns us to the most potent source of our energy: our physical and emotional connection to the earth. Even if you can't make it to the waves or the trees, you can always take time to return to the elements. Take a bath in warm water, cuddle with a furry creature, let the sun warm your skin, or consciously breathe in and out for a time.

TODAY'S ACTION

Close your eyes and envision yourself floating in the waves or resting in the shade of a tree. Make it as vivid and real as possible. Let your mind quiet and your heart be full.

What I wanted was to be allowed to do the thing in the world that I did best—which I believed then and believe now is the greatest privilege there is. When I did that, success found me.
—Debbi Fields

What do you do best? Are you allowing yourself to do it? Your gift is something that comes naturally and flows from you like a river.

Maybe someone has told you that you can't or shouldn't do this thing you love, or that it is a waste of your time. Maybe you have told *yourself* that, and have spent time and energy doing other things instead of following a path that brings you joy, whether it's a career path, a hobby, or even a way of being. When you stop trying to mentally figure out what your best skills are and simply witness the qualities and actions that naturally emerge from within you, you'll find the key to your success.

TODAY'S ACTION

I give myself permission to share with the world what I do best.

*I look around and see so much fear, people getting more
and more comfortable with their hate, more at ease being
mean, more united in their separation. And I think, NO.
Not me. I will not get lost in this fearful world . . . I will
continue to be brave and kind. I will speak for real unity.
And no matter what, I will never stop loving.*
—Scott Stabile

Love is the strongest power in the universe. Love is what propels us, directs us, feeds and nourishes us. Love will change the world, and can heal all of the pain in it. How? When we have love for ourselves, we respect ourselves so much that we won't let others harm us. Then, as that love builds, it overflows and encompasses others so much that we won't let them be hurt either. If every person loved themselves to overflowing, there would be no need for war or pain, because love would prevent anyone from ever having the desire to harm another human. This is the great work of our lives.

TODAY'S ACTION

Ask yourself, what can I do today to make the world a brighter, more hopeful place? How can I cultivate and share love with others?

It's a transformative experience to simply
pause instead of immediately filling up space.
—Pema Chödrön

Do you ever find yourself running from one event to the next, one soccer game or laundry day or work call to the next and the next and the next . . . and then at the end of the day realize that your schedule was so jam-packed you didn't take even a minute to pause and reflect? It's easy to lose touch when we're too busy. What's more, when we cram ourselves full of stimuli, we leave very little room for new thoughts, emotions, and experiences to come into our sphere naturally.

Inserting a pause between activities can bring you back to the present moment. You don't have to drop everything. A pause can be as short as a single breath. If you are uncomfortable in the pause, investigate it. If you are joyful, relish it.

TODAY'S ACTION

Try putting a pause between the activities you do today. Fill these pauses with breath, compassion, and patience. Notice how your day changes.

We know the truth by the way it feels.
—Monica Kade

When we lie to someone, even if we feel it's justified, it usually doesn't feel very good. The same thing goes for when we lie to ourselves. Maybe there's a tightness in the chest or belly, a dry mouth, or even the fuzzy-headedness that comes with trying to keep all the lies straight.

The truth doesn't feel like that. The truth feels calm, centered. And the body feels open and unguarded, even when telling the truth is uncomfortable or scary.

While you can certainly know the truth logically, you can also train yourself to *feel* the truth. Feeling the truth is when your first impression about a person or situation turns out to be right on. It's the truth that lives in your gut, your bones, and your heart. Feel it.

TODAY'S ACTION

Try speaking truths and lies out loud and notice how they feel different in your body. Then whenever you feel those physical symptoms come up in your daily life, you can use them to track your thoughts back to the original truths or lies. You'd be amazed how often it can be that we lie to ourselves until we become aware of exactly what a lie feels like.

The things you are passionate about
are not random, they are your calling.
—Fabienne Fredrickson

Today, many people identify themselves with what they do for a living. For instance, you might say, "I am an accountant" rather than "I work in accounting." What we do to make money often equates with who we are, whether that's what we're passionate about or not.

Sometimes we allow our profession or responsibilities to close off access to our true passions. But the things we are passionate about set our heart free, and sharing our passions is how we make real connections with one another. Don't define yourself by what you do to put food on the table; define yourself instead by the things that enliven you and stoke your inner fire.

TODAY'S ACTION

If someone asks you what you do, try substituting your passions for your job: "I *am* a passionate painter! My *job* is as a dentist." And instead of asking people what they do for a living, ask them what they are passionate about.

When you say "yes" to the "isness" of life, when you accept this moment as it is, you can feel a sense of spaciousness within you that is deeply peaceful.
—Eckhart Tolle

So much of our lives is spent planning for the future and thinking about the past. Yet neither of those states *is*. Only one thing is happening *right now*—the present moment. And while the present moment may feel too small and too fleeting to commit to, saying yes to what is brings us as much space and time as we will ever need. For the present is always available, never ending, and continually unfolding. So say yes to this moment. Go even further by saying yes to yourself, exactly as you are. It takes practice to say yes to life, and a willingness to let go of the notion that you must change in some way to find peace. Go toward the peace now and open up the space of yes.

TODAY'S ACTION

Start small. What can you say yes to today that you might normally try to fix or resist?

Being an intellectual creates a lot of questions and no answers. You can fill your life up with ideas and still go home lonely. All you really have that really matters are feelings. That's what music is to me.

—Janis Joplin

The thinking mind's job is to think, which is only a small part of what we need in life. Our thinking mind won't help us experience emotion without judgment, or find our inner stillness, or feel the needs of our bodies. When we rely mostly on our intellect, we step onto a never-ending mental treadmill of trying to figure things out.

One way to step out of this is to pay attention to your feelings. Name them, and let them guide you. If you find yourself judging them or shutting down joy, or grace, or even anger—I invite you to release and let go.

TODAY'S ACTION

Your feelings are like a favorite eccentric aunt who wears soft jewel-toned scarves and writes poetry on the walls. Who lets each feeling pass like a storm moving across a blue sky. Imagine yourself spending time with her wildness as she teaches you to dance to every genre of song, in any kind of weather.

Growth is painful. Change is painful. But nothing is as painful as staying stuck somewhere you don't belong.
—Mandy Hale

Change is inevitable and constant, and fighting against the inevitable always leads to suffering. The next time you're faced with a life change, rather than resisting, embrace the change and move through it consciously. This doesn't mean you want the change, or that you prefer it, but rather that you understand it's coming whether you like it or not, and you make a decision to pull yourself into alignment with life. In this way, you won't stay stuck in a rut, and the pain of change and growth will ease because you tackle it on your own terms and in your way, armed with the knowledge that it only hurts as much as you allow it to.

TODAY'S ACTION

Think about an area of your life where you are resisting change. Maybe it's making a change in your career, planning a move to a new home, or changing a relationship that isn't serving you. What's the first step you can take to embrace this change instead of resisting it?

At the end of it all, what flashes before our eyes won't be all the things we did that were bigger than ourselves; they'll be all the moments when we made a difference by being true to ourselves.
—Lori Deschene

Our culture bombards us with the expectation that we should be larger than life, picture perfect, and generally impressive at all times. It's easy to fall into the trap of believing that our true purpose should be tied to being well known or to making huge gestures that people will remember for generations to come. But when you interact with the world in a way that is real and true to who you are, you'll find that's when you are most connected to yourself and your fellow human beings. You can make more of an impact through thoughtful, one-on-one conversations than you can by getting your name in the spotlight. These little moments of truth demand our attention and authenticity in real time, and also give us the greatest reward when we manage to stay steadfast in who we are.

TODAY'S MANTRA

I stand steady and firm in who I am. My truth is valid and loving. I share my truth generously with my fellow beings.

To communicate through silence is
a link between the thoughts of man.
—Marcel Marceau

We live in an age where people are constantly on the go, and the sheer volume of communication overshadows the value of real human contact. Most people would look at you like you were crazy if you suggested they take time to communicate through silence. But that's just what I suggest in my workshops, where I have people pair up and look into each other's eyes.

Communicating through silence can feel like an abrupt shift. Most pairs' first reaction is to giggle; it feels silly. Then, as the stare continues, it grows more uncomfortable because we become more vulnerable and we see another human's vulnerability as well. Some people even begin to cry. Silence can be one of the most profound forms of communication. No words need to be spoken to share love, compassion, and empathy.

TODAY'S ACTION

Take a few minutes to get still, quiet the mind, and surrender to the universe. Notice the communication that reaches you in silence.

If you are unhappy with anything . . . whatever is bringing you down, get rid of it. Because you'll find that when you're free, your true creativity, your true self comes out.
—Tina Turner

In order to bring in the new, we must release the old. Sometimes we know just what we need to release, but other times the distinction can be hard to spot. For instance, while it's easy enough to declutter a closet, we may not be able to or want to "get rid of" certain people in our lives. However, we can get rid of our ideas about who others should be and how they should act. After all, we have no control over someone else—only our own thoughts and actions. Our ideas about what's best for others can make us unhappy, especially when others don't agree with our perspective. To bring in the new, we need to be willing to create space, and then trust. In the mysterious gap where the old and the new don't yet meet—this is where the magic happens.

TODAY'S MANTRA

I will release whatever is bringing me down today, including my thoughts about what others should be doing in their lives.

I know God will not give me anything I can't handle.
I just wish that He didn't trust me so much.
—Mother Teresa

S ometimes it feels that our experiences are too much to handle . . . that we've been given too much sorrow, too much hurt, or too much pain to hold. When your burdens feel unbearable, remind yourself that the universe is helping you hold the weight. You can allow yourself to feel how difficult this moment is. After all, pretending it isn't hard will most likely just compound the pain. But it can help to remember that the world is not punishing you; the Divine will never abandon you. Your inner trials are the very grounds for a Warrior Goddess in training to grow the muscles of compassion and the mind-set of fierce love.

TODAY'S MANTRA

I am a Warrior Goddess. I am growing and expanding every day.

People become attached to their burdens sometimes
more than their burdens are attached to them.
—George Bernard Shaw

What burdens are you grasping with both hands? When you criticize yourself for your past mistakes or worry incessantly about future fears, your mind acts like Velcro, catching every negative thought and adding more weight to your load.

Notice how these burdens start to form a part of your identity. "I shouldn't have done that," or "I am afraid XYZ will happen," are statements that, if repeated enough, become beliefs that you attach to. And you carry these worries in your mind even when they aren't relevant to the present moment. The result of all that holding on can be that we become the central victim in our mind's tale of woe. What would your life be like if you weren't fixated on your burdens?

TODAY'S ACTION

Name one of the mental burdens you are carrying and say out loud, "I release this!" Shake your body to clear the sticky Velcro. Imagine wearing a beautiful dress of spun gold that provides a magical barrier between you and the burdens of your past and your worries of the future.

Feelings are just visitors, let them come and go.
—Mooji

Sometimes we can become so identified with a feeling that we confuse it for being a part of who we are, rather than energy that is passing through us. Even our language works against us in this way, equating our being with a feeling. For instance, we'd probably say "I am sad," rather than the more accurate "there are feelings of sadness inside me right now," or "I am feeling sad right now." The distinction here is key, because if we equate certain emotions with who we are, we begin to incorporate those feelings into our personal story. If we tell ourselves enough times "I am sad," then we can more easily believe the story that "my life is sad." Remember, your emotions are both wonderful gifts and powerful tools for discerning your inner truth, but they are not who you are.

TODAY'S ACTION

Whatever emotions you experience today, try to notice them from a place of detached observation. You can feel the feelings while remembering that they are not who you are.

*Get rid of clutter and you may just find that it
was blocking the door you've been looking for.*
—Katrina Mayer

So often decisions overwhelm us because there are multiple actions we can take. Which one is right? Which path will reflect my heart's desire? In order to see all the doorways of potential, we need an uncluttered view. Physical and mental clutter often piles up because we are resisting letting go of our "shoulds" and our "somedays."

Today, make some simple decisions to let go or take one step forward. Recycle the cracked vase, give away old clothes, and drop any ideas that you should be any other way than how you are right now. Once this is done, you will have a clear view of the millions of doorways open to you.

TODAY'S ACTION

Sometimes when your mind is feeling cluttered, it helps to clear your physical space. Tidying up your desk, putting away the dishes, and folding the laundry are all good ways to put your brain to work, which can bring inspiration on how to declutter your internal space as well.

Sometimes questions are
more important than answers.
—Nancy Willard

Paying attention to the questions you ask your-self can be a spiritual practice in and of itself. For instance, questions such as "Why is this happening to me?" or "Why do I always do this?" often have self-judgment built right into them, and as a result they make us feel bad rather than help us find the answer to any challenge we are experiencing. Simply chang-ing the focus of our questions can open up whole new avenues of compassion for ourselves and provide a way forward through our darkest moments. Be aware of your intention, and let your questions flow in a way that is curious, loving, and healing.

TODAY'S ACTION

Try on these questions when faced with challenges: What will best support me in this situation? What do I really want here? How would I act if I weren't afraid?

When I let go of what I am, I become what I might be.
When I let go of what I have, I receive what I need.

—Lao Tzu

It is so easy to want to grasp, to hold tight, or to try to bind what we love to us. But grasping comes from the fear that we will lose something we have or not get something we want.

You can't become who you are meant to be if you're clinging to who you think you should be. You can't get what you need if you're clinging to what you think you want. To rest into infinite wisdom, you need to let go and trust that everything is unfolding exactly as it should.

While letting go begins with things on the outside, it also applies to your inner journey. When you let go of who you think you are, of what you think you want, or of trying to control what may or may not happen, then Life brings you what you need and reminds you who you truly are.

TODAY'S ACTION

What are you holding today that you need to let go of? It could be a possession, an idea, a demand you have on someone else, or a role you are playing that is no longer helpful. Let it go and see what happens.

The quieter you become, the more you can hear.
—Ram Dass

Our minds are constantly running, constantly weaving stories about everything around us. It's not just a dog on the sidewalk; it's a dog that snuck out of its fence and whose owners are looking for it. It's not just a new car parked across the street; it's the neighbor's illicit lover we've never seen before. Our friend didn't just forget to call; they have betrayed and abandoned us.

We make up stories about everything—it's a habit of the mind—but these stories are not reality. The truth is, as far as we are aware, without creating any stories around these observations, it's just a dog. It's just a new car. It's just our friend being busy. When we become aware of our stories, we can turn down the volume on them. Aside from quieting the constant chatter, silencing the stories allows us to make room to hear the truth of what's really going on.

TODAY'S ACTION

Practice meditation for five, ten, or thirty minutes (whatever you feel you can manage). Your mind will not be silent right away. Notice when your mind begins to get lost in a story, and gently redirect it back to stillness, back to focusing on your breath.

Give yourself permission to immediately walk
away from anything that gives you bad vibes.
—Sonia Choquette

On the Warrior Goddess path, we value our intuition as much as our logical mind. In a world where so much credence is given to physical, hard evidence, we often forget that we have our own lie detectors right in our gut. Some scientists are even starting to call the gut the "second brain."

Regardless of what you call it, our intuitive side is always available to us if we are willing to listen.

TODAY'S ACTION

To get more in tune with your intuition, start keeping an intuition journal. On one side, write the date and what you felt (or intuited). Capture as many of these sparks of intuition as you can. Then when you hear something that makes you go "I knew it!" write down the outcome across from your original feeling. This will help you develop your intuitive sense by validating the ways it appears in your everyday life.

You and I are essentially infinite choice-makers. In every moment of our existence, we are in that field of all possibilities where we have access to an infinity of choices.
—Deepak Chopra

If you knew you were infinite spaciousness in a world of all possibilities, what would you choose to create for yourself? If there were no limitations, what would you dream? Expanding your vision allows miracles to happen in the spaciousness. There is real power in creative visualization, in the process by which you visualize in your mind's eye the things that you want for yourself. Too many times we don't do this because of old self-limiting beliefs that say "That isn't possible for me," or "I don't deserve that." You are entitled to good things; and seeing them as a possibility is the first step to experiencing them.

TODAY'S ACTION

Take a few moments and visualize yourself receiving or achieving the good that you want, including fulfilling relationships, inner peace, as well as material possessions and financial gain. Notice if the mind says things like, "It's selfish to want those things," or "We can't always get what we want." Gently remind yourself that you have a direct line to infinity.

*I think it's important to realize you can
miss something, but not want it back.*
—Paulo Coelho

Humans have the incredible ability to experience multiple emotions at the same time. For instance, we can feel both sadness and gratitude simultaneously. Sometimes, even when we know we have done the right thing in releasing a particular relationship, desire, or belief, we can feel a twinge of longing, or an emptiness in that area of our lives. That's okay. You can miss the things you lose or choose to let go of, and continue to release them.

TODAY'S ACTION

Write down one thing that you are truly ready to release. Crumple the paper up and hold it in your hand. Hold it tightly, crush it against your heart, and whisper your goodbyes. Express any gratitude you have for the lessons you've learned or the feelings you've experienced connected to this thing. Now open your hand and let it fall into a cleansing flame or wastebasket and know that it is gone.

*The word is a force you cannot see, but you
can see the manifestation of that force, the
expression of the word, which is your own life.*
—Don Miguel Ruiz

Your word is not only what you say to others; it's the language you use with yourself. Your word is the most powerful force you have. Your word can help you manifest your dreams, or it can tear you down.

So often the voices in our head are not our true voice, but bits and pieces of our parents, friends, teachers, religious leaders, etc. that we are carrying around—sometimes for many years. Give yourself permission to let go of other people's words that have masqueraded as your own. Your job is to claim your *own* word as the most powerful force of manifestation, and let go of any words from those around you that do not serve you.

TODAY'S ACTION

Put all your focus on how you are speaking to yourself today. Take every opportunity to express your appreciation, love, support, and commitment to yourself. When you hear the voice of your internal judge, simply notice it and remind yourself that you are only expressing positively today. Speak out loud so you can hear your own words. Notice how you feel when you do so.

Embrace the glorious mess that you are.
—Elizabeth Gilbert

Every person on the planet experiences cycles of mess and magic, chaos and creativity—sometimes both at the same time! Instead of judging the messy chaos, or trying to control it, or wishing that it wasn't happening, embrace it in the moment as part of the cycle of life as a human. Besides, it is very often our inner judge who objects to our confusion and our contradictions. When we embrace our complexity as a magnificent quality instead of a limitation, the possibilities are endless. A friend once said to me: "Love the chaos and know that the creativity will follow."

TODAY'S MANTRA

The world spins out of control, and I surrender to it. I love the messy, glorious being that I am.

Change happens by listening and then starting a dialogue with the people who are doing something you don't believe is right.
—Jane Goodall

When we see people doing something we don't believe is right, the temptation is to judge them silently or confront them angrily—both expressions of our inner judge. Neither of these approaches creates transformation. When we get quiet and curious, though, and witness from a place of discernment about what we want to change, we are beginning to cultivate the patience, openness, and respect we will need to dialogue about creative possibilities. This is the realm of our inner artist, where real change occurs.

TODAY'S ACTION

Look for those times when you have judged or reacted to someone because you didn't agree with their point of view. Can you bring an attitude of curiosity to your next encounter, and release your need to change the person?

We don't see things as they are, we see them as we are.
—Anaïs Nin

Our mind is constantly creating stories about everything it perceives, and these stories are built up by our past experiences and personal agreements that we've made in our lives. When something happens, we take what we perceive with our senses and run it through our story-making brain and voilà, out pops our "reality." But this isn't reality, only our perception of it. Therefore, everything that we see is what we are, and everything that we perceive is a reflection of the agreements and beliefs that we hold inside of us.

When we remember this, it allows us to understand the actions that others take, even when we don't agree with them. We are each coming from our own story, and we can detach from our own story and those of others without demanding that everyone agree. This is often a step toward peace.

TODAY'S ACTION

Think of someone in your life who has a story about reality that you don't agree with. Can you see things from another perspective and understand how this story might be true for them at this time?

A company is only as good as the people it keeps.
—Mary Kay Ash

When you surround yourself with people who act with good intentions, you will enjoy their goodness. Of course, the opposite is also true. We can all strive to have compassion for others, but just because you have empathy for someone doesn't mean that you have to be a part of their situation—especially if the person is taking actions or speaking words that are hurtful. Love yourself enough to let go of those who don't make you feel enriched by having them in your life. Making a strong boundary about what's okay and what's not okay for you can be a powerful complement to your compassionate kindness.

TODAY'S ACTION

In your mind's eye, kindly say goodbye to those who are not helping to guide, protect, or love you while you are on this journey. If you need help letting go, hold a rock and name those you have to say goodbye to, and thank them for all the ways they have served you. Then bury the rock with the intent to release them with gratitude.

You've got to express yourself . . . what you reveal, you heal.
—Chris Martin

When we keep painful things bottled up inside us, we may think we are shielding ourselves and our loved ones. Indeed, you've probably been told to "buck up," "pull it together," or "move on." But for humans, the secret to feeling better is sharing our emotions with others. Talking about what is upsetting to us can be one of the most difficult things we do, and it is often the things we don't want to speak of that we need to talk about the most. The good news is that when we reveal our most intimate places to people we trust to love and respect us fully, then layers of hurt fall away and deep healing happens.

TODAY'S ACTION

You know that one thing that you don't want to talk about or confront at all? Today, for five minutes, you're going to face it. You can do this by practicing silent meditation, by writing a letter to yourself, or, best of all, by sharing it with a friend. Allow yourself to be vulnerable. Feel uncomfortable. This discomfort is only for a brief moment, and once you bring the issue to the surface, you can begin to heal.

Never wish them pain. That's not who you are. If they
caused you pain, they must have pain inside.
Wish them healing. That's what they need.
—Najwa Zebian

We've all been told to be the bigger person in a tough situation, to not stoop to someone else's low. But it can be a challenge to wish someone well when they've hurt us—especially if it seems like they've done it on purpose. What happens when we wish pain on other people, though, even people who have caused us pain, is that we continue to create pain inside us. When we wish hurt on another, we become the victimizers and abusers of ourselves, because we are the ones who feel the negativity. In the spirit of Warrior Goddess power and compassion, we want to move past the anger, the despair, the pain as quickly as we can, and wish healing upon the other person instead. Because when we do, not only are we helping that other person relieve their own pain, we're also healing ourselves.

TODAY'S MANTRA

May all beings be happy. May all beings find peace. This includes me.

Weeds are flowers too, once you get to know them.

—A. A. Milne

Sometimes the people we initially find difficult blossom into dear friends. The same can go for someone who is so quiet you hardly know they are there. In fact, everyone you meet has a flower hidden within, no matter how prickly or reticent they may be. Like many weeds that have medicinal properties, these dear friends may even have the exact healing qualities you've been seeking.

TODAY'S ACTION

Every person you meet today has some gift to offer you (and this is true every day). See if you can notice what the gift is, and pay particular attention to those the mind judges as unlikeable or incompatible.

We delight in the beauty of the butterfly, but rarely admit
the changes it has gone through to achieve that beauty.

—Maya Angelou

The butterfly is often a metaphor for transformation, but do you think the butterfly has it easy? It doesn't! A butterfly must break free of its cocoon on its own. If a human comes along and "helps," its wings wouldn't have the strength to lift its body off the tree branch. The wings themselves must be strengthened as they work to push out of the cocoon. It's hard, and probably even painful, for a butterfly to emerge! But each push of a delicate wing makes it stronger so that when it does spring free, it's able to carry itself wherever it needs to go on wings of its own.

TODAY'S ACTION

When has change been hard for you? How have you overcome those struggles to create strength inside yourself? Make a mental list of the things you've found hard to change, and give yourself a well-deserved pat on the back. Remember this list anytime you feel like change might be too hard or you feel yourself getting overwhelmed.

The more you praise and celebrate your life,
the more there is in life to celebrate.
—Oprah Winfrey

I think of my voice and my actions together as my megaphone. When I have a thought, if I speak about it or take action on it, I make it real and bring it out into the world. Because of this, I want to make sure that the thoughts I bring to life with my words and actions are the ones that are going to serve me best.

There are no better thoughts and actions than those that express gratitude, and as you amplify an attitude of gratitude with your own joyful megaphone, you draw more of that loving, positive energy into your world.

TODAY'S ACTION

Even a "bad" thought (there's no such thing, they're just thoughts) can be turned on its head as you bring it into the world. For instance, the thought "Shit! I forgot to go to the grocery store," can become, "Time for a surprise adventure to the grocery store!" At first, it may sound strange or silly to make a positive from a negative, but the more you work at it, the easier it will become. And the more you'll actually believe it when you give a situation a positive spin.

You may encounter many defeats, but you must not be defeated. In fact, it may be necessary to encounter the defeats, so you can know who you are, what you can rise from, how you can still come out of it.

—Maya Angelou

The path to personal freedom is full of distractions. Defeats in our lives, or what I call obstacles, are not meant to destroy us but to strengthen us. Each challenge helps us find the courage to go on. Each difficult encounter gives us the opportunity to discover our strength and wisdom. Each knock in the dirt offers fresh perspective on ourselves and our surroundings, if we only let it. Life is not a great mountain we climb—it is a cycle of little deaths and rebirths, defeats and triumphs. See yourself as the phoenix that rises from the ashes in a brilliant blaze of color and start using all of your defeats as rebirths.

TODAY'S ACTION

Ask a mentor or elder you respect to tell you the story of a time they were brought to their knees by a defeat. Find out how it changed them, and what gifts it brought their way.

Maybe it's animalness that will make the world right again:
the wisdom of elephants, the enthusiasm of canines,
the grace of snakes, the mildness of anteaters.
—Carol Emshwiller

One of the biggest myths created by humans is the idea that we are the most intelligent species on the planet. Sure, we've built great cities and invented marvelous technologies, but is that the only measure of intelligence? We've also built bombs and brought ecological disaster to our planet. I believe we need less human intelligence and more animal wisdom. To find balance, we need to connect to the silent knowledge of animals and plants. They remind us that we are part of something larger; that we are but a thread in a larger fabric of sky and stars and earth.

TODAY'S ACTION

Get in touch with the natural world in whatever way you can. Relish your dog's joyful discovery of the familiar. See your cat's contentment in a patch of sunlight. Or take a walk in the woods or your neighborhood and notice any critters you encounter.

When I accept myself, I am freed from the
burden of needing you to accept me.
—Steve Maraboli

Stoking your inner fire first means finding what gives you that passion within, that drive to explore, to love, to harmonize with the world. So often our inner fire is dampened by trying to be what other people expect us to be, whether it's at home, at work, within our circle of friends, or through the expectations placed on women by society at large. But the truth is that even as you search for and refine your passion, there is nothing you need to do to become the perfect version of you. You are the only one like you that has ever or will ever exist. When you accept yourself, your inner fire burns brightly and you can slough off all the detritus that has kept it shadowed. You can lay down the burden of needing someone else's approval and stand in your own truth and say, "Yes. This is me."

MANTRA

This mantra is particularly powerful if you can take some time to recite it in front of a mirror. "I am who I am. I love and accept myself for who I am. This is me."

Stay away from anyone who makes
you feel like you're hard to love.
—Holly Riordan

Why would I want to be around someone who thinks I'm difficult, cranky, stubborn, or any other kind of hard to love? Because I'm related to them? Because I've known them forever? Or maybe it's because secretly, deep down, I believe I'm hard to love.

Loving yourself isn't just a matter of saying positive affirmations while standing naked in front of the bathroom mirror. Sometimes it's respecting yourself enough to walk away from any person or situation who is judgmental of you, or who makes you feel anything less than the perfect being that you are. Some people will not be able to support you in your journey. And they're free to make that choice. It's your choice to say, "Okay. I wish you well on your own journey, but this is where our paths divide." It can be difficult to tell your mother, your sister, or your lover that you don't see the world and yourself as they do. But you can love them even as you choose another path. And remember, nothing is forever.

TODAY'S MANTRA

I will make a boundary with those whose presence does not serve my highest good. I respect everyone's choices, including my own.

Trust the still, small voice that says,
"this might work and I'll try it."
—Diane Mariechild

Sometimes the fearful voices in your mind speak so loudly that they drown out everything else. Those anxious voices often rely on "logic" to justify themselves. We all know that the loudest voice in the room is not necessarily the most creative, wise, or true. And just as in any boardroom or community meeting, it takes some care and attention to bring the quieter voices into their rightful place. Try this: Tune your ears away from the loud, critical thoughts that clamor for attention in your head. Turn down the volume of your fears and doubts. Take the microphone away from the voice of comparison. Good. Now, get quiet. Listen for the soft, small voice that knows the way.

TODAY'S ACTION

Practice listening to your inner voice by tuning your ear to the subtle sweet sounds around you: birdsong, children's laughter, the wind through the leaves. Then seek to find the song, laughter, and wind inside of you.

You alone are enough. You have nothing to prove to anybody.
—Maya Angelou

From cars to clothes to food to tampons to dating apps, so much of the way we are told to consume comes from the idea that we are not enough as we are. When we feel something is missing in us—when we agree that we are not enough, and the self-judgment and self-condemnation begin—we make perfect targets for marketers. That is the power of the agreements we make. But the truth is, you *are* enough. You have always been enough. And once you understand that your agreement with these ideas is what gives them control over you, you can say, "this isn't for me," and push them aside.

TODAY'S ACTION

Try watching a few commercials or looking at some ads in a magazine. Notice the way advertisers show that somehow you are "less than" until you buy or use their product. When you start looking at it without attachment, it becomes a fun game—it's like playing hide-and-seek with the hidden meanings, and each time you can stop and say, "Oh! You almost got me!"

The best way to find out if you can
trust somebody is to trust them.
—Ernest Hemingway

If we've been hurt in the past, we can wall ourselves off in certain areas. The pain of a loss or betrayal can feel so unbearable that we never want to give anyone the power to hurt us again. But the only way to know if someone is going to hurt you is simply to let go, and be open to the possibility. Yes, you may get hurt again; but walling yourself off without true intimacy is just as painful. When we shut down our ability to trust, we also close off access to all the emotions that enrich our lives most: love, joy, connection.

TODAY'S ACTION

Look at where you've been holding yourself back in relationships. Be honest: Are you holding back because you truly believe this person is going to harm you, or because of armoring from previous wounds? If it's the former, maybe you should consider letting go—but if it's the latter, this is a chance for you to work on breaking down walls and letting someone in.

There are two basic motivating forces: fear and love.
When we are afraid, we pull back from life. When
we are in love, we open to all that life has to offer
with passion, excitement, and acceptance.
—John Lennon

We often armor our hearts and become hesitant in our loving due to traumatic or difficult events from the past. It takes great courage to turn toward love when fear is grasping our ankles and constantly reminding us of the past. It may feel counterintuitive, but don't try to ignore or punish your fear. Like a child in need of extra loving attention, it will only get louder and more insistent. Instead, remind it gently but firmly that it is no longer in charge, and that love is taking the lead.

TODAY'S ACTION

Gently take fear by the hand and tell it you know it is scared. Thank it for its efforts to try to protect you from pain. You can even give it some loving reflections such as "I know this worries you a lot," or "It's hard to believe that you can trust again." Then, ask fear to hold hands with its big sister, love. Let love teach fear how to be brave.

Don't you dare, for one second, surround yourself with
people who are not aware of the greatness that you are.
—Jo Blackwell-Preston

As women, we often put a lot of pressure on ourselves to make sure other people see us in a certain light, whether it's perfect and pristine, or wild and inviting. While there's certainly nothing wrong with wanting to make a good impression or put your best foot forward, we often allow these expectations to color what we think about ourselves. Or we resign ourselves to the confines of a box we're supposed to fit into that can never contain the whole of our infinite and glorious selves. I truly believe that it's important to surround yourself with people who support you, who lift you up, and who honor your wholeness—but by that same token it's just as important to be that person for yourself. More than anyone else, *you* are the one who needs to be aware of the greatness that you are.

TODAY'S MANTRA

I am aware of the greatness that I am.

A crown, if it hurts us, is not worth wearing.
—Pearl Bailey

One of the things we learn on the Warrior Goddess path is what is meant for us and what is not. So many of us were told who to be, what we like, and what we should be doing or acquiring that we get out of touch with who we really are and what we really want. Just as no two women have the same body or mind, no two of us value the same things. Too often we embrace what we think everyone else wants, discarding our true feelings. We accept wearing a cumbersome crown on our heads because it is powerful or beautiful, or because it makes us feel important. We tell ourselves that whatever pain it causes is worth bearing. Why? Let it go.

TODAY'S ACTION

Are you maintaining something in your life at the insistence of others rather than your own true desires? It might be a relationship, a professional pursuit, or some possession that serves as a status symbol. Noticing what no longer serves your current heart's desire is the first step to letting it go.

The expressive body is not literal; it's very primal, and that's what I feel like when I make the best of my work. It's coming from a primal place rather than an intellectual place.
—Michael Leunig

Think back to a time you wrote or made something you're really proud of. Were you in the zone, away from the surface of day-to-day thoughts and plumbing the depths of your emotions and intuition? To get to this place, you have to move beyond the logical, judging mind, with all its ideas of right and wrong, good and bad, what will work and will not work. The logical mind is a wonderful and valuable tool, but it isn't your best creative partner. Get quiet and say hello to your physical, nonverbal self. Let everything you create be birthed from the primal depths.

TODAY'S ACTION

Take at least fifteen minutes to put on music and dance around like crazy in your bare feet. I find the best songs for moving my body are those with heavy drumbeats and limited vocals or lyrics. Fifteen minutes may seem like a long time, but it's really only four or five songs. Use this precious time to reconnect with your physical being, get a little sweaty, and let your creativity flow uncensored.

Whatever human endeavor we choose,
as long as we live our truth, it is success.
—Kamal Ravikant

When it comes to dealing with others in difficult or tense situations, it's important to remember that all you can do is communicate from your truth with compassion and integrity. If it's tough for others to hear or accept your truth, that isn't your fault, and it's not on you to make them understand. All you need to do is keep living and embodying your truth. They will either accept you or they won't, but that choice is up to them, not to you.

TODAY'S MANTRA

I am satisfied and content to live my truth with integrity. The judgments of others belong to them, and I won't take them on or attach to them personally.

I paint self-portraits because I am so often alone,
because I am the person I know best.
—Frida Kahlo

No matter who you are, where you go, what you're doing, or who you surround yourself with, at the end of the day there's only one person who is always there when you open your eyes, and only one person who is with you when you close them at night: you. Many of us don't spend much time getting to know that person; we would rather focus outwardly on spouses, children, family, and friends. But that person is always with you, and wouldn't you want to deeply know and understand the person you are going to be with from the beginning to the end of your life?

TODAY'S ACTION

Take some time to get to know yourself in a new way: draw or paint a self-portrait. You don't have to be any good at art—just take some time to get to know the features of your face and the coloring of your hair and eyes, not by memory but by looking deeply at yourself in a mirror or photograph. Put your self-portrait someplace safe, so that you can look at it again in a few years and notice any internal or external changes.

Seeking means: to have a goal; but finding means:
to be free, to be receptive, to have no goal.
—Hermann Hesse

M any of us spend our day in seeking mode—we want to do something, get something, accomplish something. It goes without saying that we all have to get things done in the world on a daily basis: go to the grocery store, send emails at work, pick up the kids from school, etc. But when it comes to being comfortable in our own skin, to becoming who we are meant to be, seeking doesn't apply. There is no checklist for this work. Instead, we need to practice absolute and total acceptance of who we are at this very moment. When it comes to being you, there is nowhere to go and nothing to do. How could there be? You can only find out who you really are by *being* rather than by doing.

TODAY'S ACTION

Take the next five minutes to sit quietly and accomplish nothing. Just be. When a thought arises of what you need to do later, or where you want to go, remind yourself that for the next five minutes you are just being. Listen to the noises you hear. Notice how your body feels. When a thought of doing arises, gently steer yourself back to being, and leaving the doing for later.

Most of us have two lives: the life we live,
and the unlived life within us. Between
the two stands resistance.
—Steven Pressfield

Do you have a deep-seated belief that you aren't good enough to achieve your goals? Smart enough? Talented enough? Resistance is natural, and it will take many forms: ambivalence, procrastination, even blame. In the face of resistance, you must decide it is your job, your birthright, and your deep privilege to live your unlived life, with exactly the amount of intelligence and talent you have right this moment.

TODAY'S ACTION

Think about something you really want but for whatever reason haven't pursued. This is your unlived life. Now see if you can locate your resistance—the fear or insecurity that is holding you back. Name it, thank it, and let it go.

Humans are allergic to change. They love to say, "We've always done it this way." I try to fight that. That's why I have a clock on my wall that runs counter-clockwise.

—Grace Hopper

It can feel easier to keep failing doing what we know than to succeed by trying something new. We can get so set in our routines that they become automatic habits, and this can prevent us from seeing creative solutions to problems or issues when they arise. However, even small, intentional changes to your routines can break the rut and allow for new experiences. Living this way expands the rooms we live in, and takes our focus off results and brings it back to the process. After all, process is where change really happens. As Warrior Goddesses, we pay great attention to the dangers of rote behavior, and commit to switching things up!

TODAY'S ACTION

The next time you hear someone else (or yourself) say in response to a problem, "But we've always done it this way," stop and ask yourself: "What is the opportunity here? Can I change this process or approach?" The answer is always yes.

I always prefer to believe the best
of everybody. It saves so much trouble.
—Rudyard Kipling

In my world, I see other people as innately good, but still capable of making bad decisions—rather than the other way around. This isn't to say that you shouldn't protect yourself from others' bad decisions; but when you're faced with the option of believing that someone is a "good" or "bad" person, try to believe in the good. This choice has no bearing on the other person—but it has every bearing on your own life, and on your own peaceful existence. Choose to believe that people are good because that is the world you wish to live in, and that is the one you can create for yourself.

TODAY'S MANTRA

I choose to see the good in all humankind—even the humans who make bad decisions. Every person must travel their own journey from where they are, and I honor their journey as I honor my own.

One of life's fundamental truths states, "Ask and you
shall receive." As kids we get used to asking for things,
but somehow we lose this ability in adulthood. We
come up with all sorts of excuses and reasons to avoid
any possibility of criticism or rejection.
—Jack Canfield

D
o you have a habit of not asking for people's
feedback, time, or anything else out of fear of
being rejected? Or because you think you don't deserve
it? Being receptive means giving yourself permission to
first name what you want, and then ask for it. Of course,
you may not get what you ask for—but asking certainly increases your chances. Get ready to enthusiasti-
cally embrace the yeses, and generously accept the nos.

TODAY'S ACTION

Ask, ask, ask! Commit to making no less than ten
direct requests today, big or small. Practice receiving
other people's yeses or nos with an open heart.

*My alone feels so good, I'll only have
you if you're sweeter than my solitude.*
—Warsan Shire

Many of us adopt the idea at some point in our lives that being "alone" is bad—that it means you must be unpopular, unloved, or broken in some way. But the Warrior Goddess path shows us that being alone doesn't mean any of those things. If you are like many women I have met on this journey, you'll find that the more comfortable you become with who you really are, the more you will appreciate the benefits of solitude.

Being comfortable with who you are might mean talking to yourself, reading poetry aloud to yourself, sitting alone and enjoying a dinner you've prepared just for you. You notice that you are happy in these alone moments, that you feel content, and that you feel free from having to please anyone else. When you become comfortable in who you are, you enjoy a balance between being with others and being in solitude.

TODAY'S ACTION

Take yourself out for a movie or dinner date. It's your date, so do what you want. Get the popcorn that you want because you want it—not because you're compromising with someone else's tastes. Start with dessert first because it sounds tasty. Embrace the freedom of being alone.

Courage is like—it's a habitus, a habit, a virtue: You
get it by courageous acts. It's like you learn to swim
by swimming. You learn courage by couraging.
—Mary Daly

The thought that you are courageous or not courageous is simply that—a thought. Courage doesn't show up on your doorstep and wait for you to open the door in the morning. Courage arises after you walk outside at midnight and try something new, in spite of your fear. You are courageous through your actions only, not your mind; so rather than pay attention to the story in your mind that says either "I am a courageous person" or "I am a scaredy-cat," start paying attention to your actions.

TODAY'S ACTION

Where can you practice couraging today? Is there someplace you need to speak up for yourself? Or maybe it's practicing holding back, or letting go and trusting the universe. Ask yourself what a courageous person would do in this situation, and then do it.

Blessed are the weird people, the poets, misfits, writers,
mystics, heretics, painters, and troubadours, for they
teach us to see the world through different eyes.
—Jacob Nordby

O n your inner journey, there comes a time when you realize that you have changed. It may be the result of numerous tiny happenings that you weren't conscious of at the time, or it may come like a lightning bolt on a dark and stormy night. But no matter, one day you realize that you are different, even a little weird, and that you have finally come home. You embrace yourself and realize that you are enough. You realize that you are a knobby, strange bundle of humanity and that you love this person very much.

In this moment, you notice how the parts of yourself that were always so awkward and painful have transformed into your most beautiful gifts. Pure alchemy has turned your lead into gold, as you now see the world through different eyes.

TODAY'S ACTION

Take a moment to notice the changes you've made so far. Imagine a room full of all of the misfits and artists who have ever inspired you, who have given the world their genius. Visualize them waiting to meet you in spirit. This is who you really are.

Life is a series of building, testing, changing and iterating.
—Lauren Mosenthal

To iterate means to perform or utter something repeatedly. Each day we wake up and do more or less what we did the day before: get dressed, go to work, plod through our familiar tasks without awareness. As an alternative, iteration can move us forward a little bit with every repetition. We can be like a scientist or construction worker—constantly building, testing, and changing our environment. Our raw materials are our thoughts, our actions, and the emotions that we experience as a result of both of these. As scientists, we can devise experiments to test the cause and effect relationship between what we think or do and how we feel. As construction workers, we can use every day as an opportunity to build something new, or to remodel any outdated structure in our life.

TODAY'S ACTION

Notice how you can deeply enjoy both trying new things and doing the exact same thing again and again. There is value in steady ritual and bold creativity alike—the key is to do both consciously.

Bitterness is like cancer. It eats upon the host.
But anger is like fire. It burns it all clean.
—Maya Angelou

Anger is an emotion like any other—and it's one we should feel free to express appropriately. If we refuse to express an emotion, stuff it down and hide it away, we'll only have it resurface again and again. Think of standing on the shore, trying to push waves back toward the sea. That would be hopeless, and totally exhausting. The key here is to express the anger appropriately and move through it when it arises. Let's learn to ride that wave in as much physical and mental alignment as we can, so we can feel the effects of the emotion without hurting ourselves or those around us.

TODAY'S ACTION

We don't intentionally cultivate anger, but it will arise like every other human emotion. When you feel angry, try simply stating out loud: "I am feeling angry right now." Naming the emotion can help you begin to move through it. This is something we teach and validate in little kids but too often lose sight of as adults.

I am where I am because I believe in all possibilities.
—Whoopi Goldberg

When you believe in your limitations, you make them real. The good news is, the opposite is also true: when you believe in possibilities, even if you are stuck or confused or scared, a crack opens into infinity. When you consciously set your intention to believe in possibilities and practice that on a daily basis, you are more likely to recognize and act on a new opportunity, even if it doesn't look like you thought it would. You don't need to know how things are going to work out—you just need to be willing to believe in unexpected miracles and your deepest wishes being fulfilled in surprising ways. So prove your naysayers wrong (even if that naysayer is you) and believe that getting what you want is not only possible, it's probable.

TODAY'S MANTRA

I open the door for the unexpected and the magical and look forward to seeing what possibilities play out.

Listening to your heart is not simple. Finding out who you are is not simple. It takes a lot of hard work and courage to get to know who you are and what you want.
—Sue Bender

Imagine that your mind and your heart are different radio stations playing at the same time. In any given situation, which signal do you tune into more? How much of what you hear from your mind is actually static? Discerning the meaning of your heart takes careful listening and purposeful action—it's naturally quieter than the mind. Can you tune into your deepest heart's wisdom? As you become more receptive to your heart, notice the differences in how you feel and act. Are you less quick to respond in anger? More able to work creatively? More comfortable in your own skin? Turning your receiver away from your mind makes space for the softer tune of your heart's melody.

TODAY'S ACTION

Take some time to sit silently today. See if you can pick the soft voice of your heart out of all the chatter in your mind. Practice makes it easier to pick out your heart's voice when you need to consult it.

You know it's love when all you want is that person to be
happy, even if you're not part of their happiness.
—Julia Roberts

Letting go of an idea of true love can feel hard, especially if we think it's our responsibility to make the other person happy, or if we think we can't be happy without that person in our lives in the way we'd imagined they should be. Wanting their happiness can be a sign of true love. And I also want to share the inverse of this quote: you know it is love when *you* want to be happy, even if they are not part of your happiness. True love frees you to let others go, both those who don't want to be with you and those you no longer want to be with.

TODAY'S ACTION

Is there any relationship in your life that needs to be adjusted in order to bring in more happiness? Advocate for your own happiness and the happiness of your partner. Small steps count—maybe it means you go together to a movie theater, but each of you sees the movie you want to see.

Painting is just another way of keeping a diary.
—Pablo Picasso

By expressing ourselves through a creative outlet, we have the ability to move emotions and emotional energy that may otherwise be stuck in our being. And as you continue creating and using this creative expression as a way to move emotions, you'll have a visual representation of your journey. You'll see where you felt happiest, where you felt low, and what colors, shapes, tones, and moods accompanied those areas. You'll be able to look back at your creative habits and learn how you processed your feelings, which can help you direct your path in the future. Maybe it's time to try a new creative outlet or pick up one you've left behind.

TODAY'S ACTION

What makes your soul sing? Commit today to just doing it—painting, quilting, drawing, writing, working with clay—lay in your supplies and start. Try to make it a daily habit, if you can.

We live in a wonderful world that is full of beauty, charm, and adventure. There is no end to the adventures that we can have if only we seek them with our eyes open.
—Jawaharlal Nehru

What new adventure is waiting around the corner for you? Sometimes it helps to take off your adult eyes and replace them with your little-kid eyes. Those are the eyes that can make a cardboard box into a time machine, find grand adventure hunting for lightning bugs, and see magic behind the next corner. Look for the beauty. Be charmed by the tiniest of things. And let yourself have your own personal adventure today. Adventures help us identify our routines as we break out of them, and into something exciting and new.

TODAY'S ACTION

Get lost today. Take an unfamiliar path along a walk. Drive without GPS or a specific place in mind. Stop when you see something interesting. This is especially fun to do with a friend on a bright, sunny day.

Life doesn't always present you with the perfect opportunity at the perfect time. Opportunities come when you least expect them, or when you're not ready for them. Rarely are opportunities presented to you in the perfect way, in a nice little box with a yellow bow on top.

—Susan Wojcicki

The most important thing about opportunity is that we need to have our eyes open and our hearts attuned to recognizing it. Rarely does the perfect opportunity appear right when we ordered it. More likely your opportunity will come as a stunning surprise, a chance to travel, a new job, or a big challenge. Opportunity also has a way of sneaking in after heartbreak or loss. Remember that old saying: when a door closes, a window opens. The trick is to not demand the time or place, but to always be in a space of relaxed readiness so you recognize the opportunity when it arrives.

TODAY'S MANTRA

I discover opportunity in hidden, unlikely places.

He who angers you conquers you.
—Elizabeth Kenny

When we allow ourselves to have an overwhelming emotional reaction to something that someone else does or says, we give away our power. We allow the emotion to dictate what we say and do, often with negative consequences. Whenever possible, we want our actions to come as conscious decisions, not unconscious reactions to emotional triggers. The next time someone does or says something that makes you feel like you're teetering on the edge of blowing up, try to take a step back and breathe deeply. This anger is a gift; it's showing you what you are afraid of, and what work you still need to do to come out ahead in the long game.

TODAY'S ACTION

Just for today, walk away from stressful or overwhelming situations. Deal with them later, after you've had a chance to cool down.

People from a planet without flowers would think we must be mad with joy the whole time to have such things about us.
—Iris Murdoch

Flowers, ladybugs, waterfalls, colored pencils, teapots, sheepskin rugs, glitter, hugs, good music, poetry, friendship . . . the list goes on and on of things that are beautiful, whose very existence makes us smile. Who doesn't feel better curling their bare toes on a fluffy rug—or in a field of grass just after the rain? Even in the darkest of times or the densest of cities, there are always flowers growing through the cracks and reminding us of the joy of embracing the sunshine and having our roots in the earth. But our mind is a tricky thing—it would often rather remind us that the rug needs to be cleaned, the grass needs to be mowed, the glitter needs to be swept up. If you notice this happening, this habit of seeing the problems rather than the happiness, take a moment to pause and appreciate the beauty behind it all.

TODAY'S ACTION

There are so many reasons to be happy today. Can you make a list of them? Post it somewhere you'll see it, and refer to it when you need a little happy in your grump.

It is awfully important to know what
is and what is not your business.
—Gertrude Stein

S ometimes it's easy to see what isn't our business, but it's hard to keep our fingers out of it. For instance, we may know that it's not our business to clean our sister's house, even if we think she'd feel better if we did. We know it's not our business to fix our friend's marriage. It's not our business to tell our grown daughter what to eat. We know this, even if we still struggle to keep our opinions to ourselves.

But here's where it gets tricky: it also is not your business what anyone else thinks of you. This might be a novel idea, so take a moment to consider it. What someone thinks of anything—their kids, their car, politics, religion, you—is only up to them. It has nothing to do with you. As long as you are your authentic self, with integrity and compassion, you are only ever doing the best you are capable of doing in the moment. And someone else's opinions, even if they are directed at you, are not your business. Release the idea that you need everyone to like you. You don't. That's their business, not yours.

TODAY'S MANTRA

What someone else thinks of me is not my business. I am doing my best.

Grief can be the garden of compassion. If you keep your heart open through everything, your pain can become your greatest ally in your life's search for love and wisdom.

—Rumi

Grief is not a robber, wanting to steal your happiness and well-being. Grief is a saint, patiently reminding you of the beauty and grace of being human. When you open to the holiness of grief, rather than trying to keep the protective armor around your heart intact, you'll be washed clean in the salty waters. That's hard to know or feel when we're in the throes of a great loss. Yet if we let ourselves feel the loss, cry when we feel like crying, talk to others when we feel like talking, list the gifts our lost one gave to us, our grief can teach us—what it's like to feel, to connect, to pass love along.

TODAY'S ACTION

When have you stuffed grief in the past? Do you have any unresolved feelings of loss you've been avoiding? The next time you're grieving, remember to share it, explore it, and allow it to just be until you've worked through the complex feelings.

The greatest obstacle to discovery is not ignorance—
it is the illusion of knowledge.
—Daniel J. Boorstin

Our mind can create stories that we swear are true, and that feed our victim or judge mentalities. These stories reinforce why we are sweet and innocent and the people who hurt us are evil and malicious. But some of these stories may not have happened the way we imagine they did—or they may not have happened at all. This is why it becomes so important to examine the stories that fuel our victimization; because when we can unravel a more truthful version of the story, we can take responsibility for our actions while simultaneously healing and releasing others for their roles as well.

TODAY'S ACTION

Think of a story you know well that pits you as the victim. How many facts do you know for sure? How many assumptions have you made? I'll bet you have far more story points than facts. In light of this, how might your story change?

The trouble with having an open mind, of course, is that people will insist on coming along and trying to put things in it.

—Terry Pratchett

It can sometimes be challenging to have an open, curious mind while also remaining clear on our truth. Add the opinion of others to the mix, and it can be like trying to stand up straight on a tilting floor. And others will always have their opinions: about how you should live, how you should behave, who you should marry or divorce, what you should wear or eat. When I start feeling the line blurring between my truth and someone else's thoughts and desires, I say a little mantra: "They are welcome to their opinion." You don't need to defend yourself, or explain to them why they are wrong, or make yourself wrong, or apologize for your experience. A simple, "that's not my experience" or "that's not how I see it" does wonders. Just because someone doesn't agree with you or wants you to do things differently does not mean you need to change; you can be open and decide if you agree with their thoughts or not.

TODAY'S ACTION

Be on the lookout for opportunities to live your truth. When people get pushy, smile and say, "No thank you."

Dedicate yourself to the good you deserve and
desire for yourself. Give yourself peace of mind.
You deserve to be happy. You deserve delight.
—Mark Victor Hansen

M ost women I work with hold some form of the self-limiting belief, "I don't deserve X, Y, or Z." They believe, sometimes subtly, that they don't deserve to be happy, or to experience pleasure, or to receive abundance. Sometimes this notion is rooted in deep-seated insecurities, and in others it masquerades as altruism or compassion, as in "I don't deserve to enjoy X, Y, or Z while others are suffering." Your guilt never helped anyone. Remember, you can experience good things in your life and still help others.

Instead of trying to be "good" or waiting for someone to tell you that you are "deserving," take charge. You *are* deserving. You get to take up space. You get to enjoy your body, mind, and experiences. You are a child of the Universe, and you deserve peace and contentment.

TODAY'S ACTION

Dedicate yourself to claiming the peace and delight that is your birthright. Say yes to yourself.

*Falling in love consists merely in uncorking
the imagination and bottling the common sense.*
—Helen Rowland

To me, falling in love isn't simply something that we do with other people. Love is a state of being; it's a place from which you can live wholeheartedly. In my experience, I find that all it takes to be in love is a willingness to open oneself to the feeling, a willingness to be vulnerable and imaginative, playful and unrestrained. I can fall in love with a song, with the trees around me, with the ground under my feet by bringing my attention to them and opening myself up to the fountain of love that is waiting inside me. That said, what about bottling up common sense? Do we have to do that to fall in love? Here's my take: when people say to live by common sense, they often mean the accepted way, the normal way, the safe way. I say, bottle up *that* common sense. Save it for a day you might need it, but don't let it get in the way of falling in love. And as we bring more love in, we can put more love out.

TODAY'S ACTION

Fall in love with something today. It might be the way a ray of sunshine comes in through the living room window, or that stray cat your neighbor keeps feeding—there's always something to fall in love with.

Common sense and a sense of humor are the
same thing, moving at different speeds. A sense
of humor is just common sense, dancing.
—William James

Picture this: Ms. Common Sense is a stately woman, with no hint of a smile on her face. She's all about paying the mortgage on time, getting the job done, cleaning the house, and moving step by step through her day. In comes Ms. Sense of Humor. She dances through the house, turns the music up, and laughs uproariously at her own jokes. She decides to go swimming instead of swabbing the bathroom floor. Who do you want to hang out with? Well, yes, it depends on what needs to get done. But when we play, we release ourselves from the anxieties and inhibitions of "adulthood." When we're able to joke and dance and be silly, we reconnect to the childlike part of us. To me, it *is* responsible to encourage and engage your inner child. In fact, when we can play and laugh at ourselves a bit, the necessary things that we have to deal with in order to function in the world actually become a bit more manageable.

TODAY'S ACTION

Play! Go out and throw or kick a ball around. Wildly dance to your favorite tunes. Dress up in a costume and make-believe all over the house.

*Until we can receive with an open heart, we're
never really giving with an open heart. When we
attach judgment to receiving help, we knowingly or
unknowingly attach judgment to giving help.*
—Brené Brown

If you've tied a portion of your inner worth to your ability to please others, you are also most likely blocking your ability to receive help and pleasure from other people. The truth is that you cannot fully give when you can't soften and receive. To begin undoing this, try taking compliments and being open to praise. When someone compliments you on a job well done, just say "thank you," rather than diminishing the compliment with a self-effacing comment like, "well, it wasn't a big deal." Let your ego step aside and receive these good words. Then carry that receptivity into receiving help and support with an open heart when it is offered. Don't think less of yourself because you want or need help, and don't think more of yourself when you give it. Receive help gratefully and joyfully, and give it willingly without conditions.

TODAY'S MANTRA

My heart and hands are open to give and receive love and support.

There is a thin line that separates laughter and pain,
comedy and tragedy, humor and hurt.
—Erma Bombeck

When I'm in a sad or depressed place, I try to focus on knowing that whatever I'm feeling now is temporary. I have faith that this emotion, painful as it is in the moment, will pass and good emotions will return. It can be difficult to see and believe this when you're in an especially dark place. Sometimes the only thing you can put faith in is the fact that the sun will rise tomorrow. But it will, as it has been doing for ages and ages and ages—and no matter what you're going through, the sun will rise tomorrow. Enough sunrises pass and you begin to see and feel that this situation too will pass, and new days, new sunrises, and new happinesses will come again.

TODAY'S ACTION

Where are you going to put your faith today? Will you put it in yourself and commit to acts of self-care? Will you put it in the wisdom of the universe, and trust that all that happens today is for your greatest good? Or will you simply rely on the fact that the sun will rise again tomorrow?

I find hope in the darkest of days, and focus
in the brightest. I do not judge the universe.
—Dalai Lama

It seems simple: "Don't judge the universe." Sure, of course. Why would you judge the universe? It's bigger and clearly knows better than you, right? But we *do* judge the universe anytime we argue with reality.

Don't think you've ever argued with reality? Try this test: When was the last time you said one of these phrases: "That's not the way it's supposed to be." "That's not how it is." "This shouldn't be happening."

If something is happening, then it *can* happen—and it is happening. Don't judge the universe; simply accept what is happening, and move forward. As a dear friend of mine likes to say when he finds himself in unexpected situations, "Why is this better than what I had planned?"

TODAY'S ACTION

When you feel yourself turning your judgment toward the universe, take a moment to stop and be aware. Take a deep breath and remind yourself that it is. Now what is your next step?

Self-care is never a selfish act—it is simply good stewardship.
—Parker Palmer

Webster's Dictionary defines stewardship as the careful and responsible management of something entrusted to one's care. What is more precious and immediate than this one unique life you have been entrusted with? Today take ownership of the land of you, and be the best long-vision self-care steward you can be of your mind, emotions, energy, and body. Practicing good stewardship means doing some maintenance every day. Taking good care of yourself means talking nicely to yourself, not judging, and paying attention. It means eating healthy and exercising; it means meditating. It means investing in yourself for the long haul. Pay attention, and take good care of what you have been entrusted with: you.

TODAY'S ACTION

Take a self-care inventory. Investigate where are you feeling run down, or where you are overdoing it or being hard on yourself. What would help you mend? Maybe it's a walk, some quiet time, or a healthy snack. Whatever it is, give yourself the time and space to take care of you.

My hope still is to leave the world
a bit better than when I got here.
—Jim Henson

Goals can be wonderful, useful tools. They spur us on; give us vision and drive, and a sense of accomplishment. But it's important that we remain flexible as we grow older, and our goals shift and change. If you feel like you haven't accomplished as much as you'd hoped to by a certain age, look closer. You might find that what you got was actually better than what you thought you wanted, and you simply forgot to release your earlier goal. I find that the goals that really stick with me are the ones that are closer to home, and that make me feel good. Those are also the goals that can contribute to making the world a better place.

TODAY'S ACTION

Take today to think about your goals, and try broadening them into something that can grow with you. For instance, "I want to climb Mount Everest" may become, "I want to continue to pursue grand adventures." Even if you don't make it to the summit of Everest, you're meeting your goal whenever you take a step toward any adventure, big or small.

Better do a good deed near at home
than go far away to burn incense.
—Amelia Earhart

The idea that happiness or enlightenment exists somewhere "out there" to be found always makes me laugh. I've certainly done it myself, thinking that if I just take this journey, meet this teacher, or read this book, I'll find what I'm looking for. After all, if I feel I'm missing something, it must be attainable from some source outside myself, right? But if we believe that happiness or enlightenment remain "out there," then we can use it as a way to distance ourselves from our present difficulties. Going to some far-off country to light incense won't fix the problem. The solution is to come home to ourselves.

The truth is that you already have everything you need inside your beautiful self. Yes, it may be helpful to have a teacher or guide who can help you discover it when you feel lost, but *you are enough.* Your care and attention in the here and now can do more than any far-flung journey to seek what's already tucked away within you.

TODAY'S MANTRA

No matter where I go, there I am.

It takes a great deal of bravery to stand up to our enemies,
but just as much to stand up to our friends.

—J. K. Rowling

As hard as it is to overcome our fear and stand up to people we don't know well, the process can be even more difficult when it comes to our close friends and family. We often retreat into tact and diplomacy— sometimes to the point of not saying anything at all.

Be careful not to sacrifice yourself on the altar of peace. If there's something you need to say to someone close to you, by all means, do so. You don't have to abandon kindness in order to be honest with those you care about. In fact, speaking your truth with bravery will often bring you closer to others by allowing them to see your authentic self. And if you've taken that courageous step and they can't accept your honesty, it's also okay to decide to walk away.

TODAY'S ACTION

Is there someone you need to stand up to or level with? Consider that you are not bringing peace to either of you by staying quiet out of habit or fear of change. Call up your bravery from the solid earth beneath your feet, and express your truth with kindness.

We shall never know all the good that a simple smile can do.
—Mother Teresa

D id you know that smiling has been scientifically proven to improve your mood, relieve stress and pain, and lower blood pressure? Those are just the benefits to you yourself. When you share a smile with someone else, they also get a boost, whether they smile back or not. You have shown your inner light by the smile on your lips, and spreading that light is how we effect positive change in the world. It may seem like an insignificant thing, but you never know how many people's days might be improved by seeing your smile.

TODAY'S ACTION

Close your eyes, and take a moment to bring to mind someone who fills your heart with joy. It could be a child, your best friend, or a beloved pet. Imagine them smiling at you, beaming love in your direction. Allow yourself to be warmed in the glow, and for a smile to let loose on your own face. Carry that feeling into your day, and smile!

Figure out who you are separate from your family, and the man or woman you're in a relationship with. Find who you are in this world and what you need to feel good alone.
—Angelina Jolie

When you are in a relationship, especially if you have children and have been partnered for a long time, it can be challenging to know who you are separate from your identity as a mom and partner. Just as you are not your profession, the essence of you is not defined by your relationships. For your mental and emotional health, as well as the health of your family, take some time to get to know who you are.

Your likes and dislikes, your passions, and how you move through the world change over time. Who you are in your twenties is different from your thirties, which is different from your forties—and each of these iterations is *you*. By connecting to and nourishing your self, you will be more present, loving, and available to others.

TODAY'S ACTION

Put a self-date on your calendar to do something strictly for you, whether it's something you just enjoy for the sheer pleasure of it or something to help you get to know yourself better. Repeat regularly.

The right to happiness is fundamental.
—Anna Pavlova

That may not sound like a radical statement—sure, everyone should be happy—but do we really mean everyone? The bully who beat you up in the third grade? That political opponent you can't stand? What about the person who broke your heart?

That's where it gets radical—with the people we don't think deserve happiness. Take a moment to feel the truth of this in your bones. Everyone is coming into this world and doing the best they can. Everyone is on a different spiritual level, and sometimes this can cause them to act in ways that bring pain or suffering to others. They may not ever feel sorry, or even know that what they did was wrong. Wishing pain back on them does nothing to help you; it only renews your sense of victimhood every time you think of them. Let go of any ties to hatred so that you too can experience this fundamental right of happiness.

TODAY'S MANTRA

With happiness, I offer forgiveness. With forgiveness, I receive happiness.

Create the kind of self that you will be happy to live with all your life. Make the most of yourself by fanning the tiny, inner sparks of possibility into flames of achievement.

—Golda Meir

It takes great bravery to take ownership of your life and choose how you want to live it. If you imagine yourself an artist and the story of your life your masterpiece, it becomes exciting to experiment, explore, and create new ways of being, thinking, and doing. Listen to your heart; it will tell you where it wants to go. And then give it a little breath—fan the flames just a bit. You don't have to change everything in your life—just ask yourself how you can find creative ways to be fully *you* within your current reality. When you're ready to go a step further, pick a small spark and give it a little nudge toward growing into a fuller flame.

TODAY'S ACTION

In the Toltec tradition, we are all artists creating the masterpieces that are our lives. How can you achieve the next level of brave creativity in your own masterpiece? What little or big changes can you initiate today that will make you feel creatively *you?*

Sexy and smart are not oil and water.
You don't have to dumb yourself down to be cute.
—Pink

Sometimes in our black-or-white, good-or-bad brains we decide that we can't be smart and sexy, or confident and humble, or excited and calm. Our brains aren't necessarily wired to appreciate when things are mismatched. We gravitate toward a certain amount of order and predictability. Plus, our culture of marketing and sales is built on known products and known consumers. But you know what? You are a marvelous mix of seemingly divergent qualities. And this is precisely what makes you interesting. You can blend any qualities however you want—and your confidence in the resulting expression of your inner light will take you far.

TODAY'S ACTION

What would excited calm look like? How would it feel to be confident and humble? How do smart and sexy blend in your being? Let go of all rules and explore how your seemingly disparate qualities can also be very connected.

I think the secret to happiness is having
a Teflon soul. Whatever comes your way, you
either let it slide or you cook with it.
—Diane Lane

When difficulties come up in our lives, we have a choice: we can let them stick to us, where they can burn and stink up situations further down the line; or we can decide to let things slide off, and stop taking them personally. We can shake the pan, add some salt or spice, and find out how to make a new dish with the wonky ingredients that have been thrown at us. Some things are meant to evolve us, and others are not ours to pick up. Knowing the difference is key.

TODAY'S ACTION

What are some things you've been holding on to that you need to let slide? Let them slide. Now, what can you cook with? Where do you need to take action in a creative or new way? The key is in bringing these two qualities together, so you let go of what is not yours and deal with what is.

People think that their world will get smaller as they
get older. My experience is just the opposite. Your senses
become more acute. You start to blossom.

—Yoko Ono

Society reminds us all too often that at some point we will become "over the hill," or that soon enough our "best days are behind us." But what if the peak of your life, that explosion of color and scent and beauty, isn't when you are twenty or thirty or forty, but seventy instead—or ninety? The idea of being past our prime or a fading blossom might be all around us, but it's simply not the truth. As we live, we continue to grow, to expand in complexity, and to deepen our understanding. We can shake our metaphorical flower booty as long as we choose to.

TODAY'S MANTRA

With each passing day, I blossom more fully into the person I am meant to be.

It's not your job to like me, it's mine.
—Byron Katie

Here are two false beliefs that many women cling to: "I must make other people like me so I feel better about myself," and a corollary to that, "If you don't like me, something must be wrong with me." The underlying belief that fuels both of these is the idea that we can and should control how we are perceived, and how others behave. As I break free of false beliefs, I've found it incredibly helpful to give others permission to like me or not like me. In the process, I relinquish the idea that I get to control them. The truth is they are going to like me or not like me regardless of what I want. I am only the boss of me. My job is to like myself and stay connected to my own kindness, humility, and joy.

TODAY'S ACTION

Write down the list of things you are the boss of. Is managing how you are seen and valued by others on your list? Even in some sneaky way? Cross it off. Control cannot foster love and appreciation—not in you, and not in your loved ones.

There are those who say fate is something beyond our command.
That destiny is not our own, but I know better. Our fate lives
within us, you only have to be brave enough to see it.
—Merida (from the film *Brave*)

Fate is like a seed within us, waiting patiently for the rains. Our bravery waters this seed of fate, so that it unfurls and begins to push through the mud and stretch toward the sun. In this way, our fate is predetermined only insofar as it is a kernel of possibility. The end result is a mystery. How your fate unfolds—its health, speed, longevity, usefulness in the world—are at your command, and belong to you. Think of the oak tree contained in the acorn: a massive organism, member of a family, home to other creatures and plants, shade provider, soil protector. Everything is already there, but it takes the right conditions to bring the tree into its fullness.

TODAY'S ACTION

See your acts of bravery as little seeds that will allow your fate to grow into the tree that will shade and nourish those who come after you. What brave actions will you take today? What will they set in motion? Meditate or journal to help you discover and nurture your seeds.

God could not be everywhere, and therefore he made mothers.
—Rudyard Kipling

Women have always held an essential role as mothers—certainly as mothers of children, but in many other ways as well. We are often nurturers and supporters of family members, friends, and communities, sometimes strangers and animals, and the planet as a whole. We use our mothering skills to help others and to co-create with Mother Earth herself. Our mothering takes shape in how we interact with other people, how we use our voices to stand up for what is right, and how we protect and care for those around us. We women are the mothers of the whole world: caretakers and guardians, guides and teachers.

TODAY'S ACTION

Think of the things that you have "birthed" into existence (think beyond children for now). What systems or dreams or creations have you brought into the world? It could be a piece of art, a new business, something you made by hand, or even a unique way to guide others to their answers. What else would you like to give birth to and nurture in the world today?

Expose yourself to your deepest fear. After that, fear has no power, and fear of freedom shrinks and vanishes. You are free.
—Jim Morrison

I once met a woman at a firewalk who decided to celebrate her seventieth year on the planet doing things that had previously terrified her: she skydived, got a tattoo, and walked on hot coals. She spent an entire year pushing her boundaries and challenging herself. I can only imagine how free she must have felt each night she went to bed having done something she had previously felt too afraid to try. There is no fear we cannot face and nothing we cannot do (in some form or another). If we take away the power fear holds over us, we are limitless.

TODAY'S ACTION

Make a list of the impossible things that you want to accomplish—things you're afraid to do. You don't have to do any of them—yet—but keep coming back to your list. When you feel ready, take the plunge. Remember, you may be scared even when you are ready; but the difference is that when you're ready, you are afraid and still willing to proceed, rather than being afraid and hiding in old patterns.

Your intuition will tell you where you need to go; it will connect you with people you should meet; it will guide you toward work that is meaningful for you—work that brings you joy, work that feels right for you.
—Shakti Gawain

I magine your intuition as a friend. Are they your bestie? Or someone you are estranged from and with whom you are hoping to reconnect? Befriending your intuition means learning to trust the sometimes quirky or confusing or nonsensical requests it makes. Be willing to follow the quiet voice of your intuition, which never demands or defends, but simply reaches out a hand and says quietly: here is your next step.

TODAY'S ACTION

Take some time today to rekindle your relationship with your intuition. The most active way is to follow its lead. Intuition says to take a walk around the block? Do it. Intuition says to cancel a plan with friends and stay in, or to call up the girls and make a date to hang out? Why not? Listen to your intuition, and then take action on that guidance.

The success of every woman should be the inspiration to another. We should raise each other up. Make sure you're very courageous: be strong, be extremely kind, and, above all, be humble.

—Serena Williams

When you see another woman who is fulfilling her dreams, what's your internal dialogue sound like? Is it something like, *I wish I was successful like her, but I am not as good as she is,* or is it, *I love that she's successful, and I'm inspired by her to become better myself?*

Focus on celebrating other women's accomplishments while you keep your attention on growing your own courage, kindness, and humility. Society often pits us against one another by encouraging comparison, but we always have the choice to participate in this or not.

TODAY'S ACTION

Notice when you are comparing yourself to other women in a way that tears yourself down, or minimizes their successes. Multiple times a day, take a moment to name something you excel at—smiling at coworkers, doing Sudoku puzzles, solving difficult technical issues, changing diapers. Remember, you are no better and no worse than anyone else.

Forgiveness is not always easy. At times, it feels more painful than the wound we suffered, to forgive the one who inflicted it. And yet, there is no peace without forgiveness.

—Marianne Williamson

When someone wounds us with their words or actions, it is tempting to keep ourselves closed and hold tightly to the pain and hurt. Sometimes we need to go within and tend to our wounds, but we have to take care that we don't add more poison to the cut through blame and judgment of ourselves. Take your time to heal by nurturing and loving yourself, and then, when you are ready, grab the hand of forgiveness. If you feel yourself attaching to blame and guilt when you try to forgive others, see if you're still holding on to blame for yourself. It's impossible to completely forgive others if you are blaming and judging yourself.

TODAY'S ACTION

Your goal is to be able to bring any person from your past into your mind, including anyone who has harmed you or hurt you in the past, and not feel any negativity toward them or yourself. You may find you still have more forgiveness work to do, and that's okay. Keep moving toward forgiveness, even if it's just a little at a time.

I just love bossy women. I could be around them all day. To me, bossy is not a pejorative term at all. It means somebody's passionate and engaged and ambitious and doesn't mind leading.

—Amy Poehler

Let's take a cue from Amy and reclaim the word bossy. Let's sing it to the rafters, launch it as a compliment, and own it for ourselves. Bossy babes unite! Imagine the best boss ever: someone who's not afraid to lead, not afraid to make mistakes and share their struggle and learning process. Someone who can inspire and help others grow with compassion and playful enthusiasm. A woman whose ambition and sense of purpose unify her team while valuing their differences. Now don't *you* want to be a bossy woman, too?

TODAY'S ACTION

Zero in on the most passionate, ambitious leader you can think of. Listen to a podcast featuring them, or read an interview or biography, and make a note every time you're excited by their "bossy" behavior.

There is a Fountain of Youth: It is your mind,
your talents, the creativity you bring to your life
and the lives of the people you love.
—Sophia Loren

Like so many things, what you seek outside your-self can only be found within. Instead of being anxious about wrinkles, or thinking your best years are behind you, get curious about what it means to be youthful on the inside. In my view, getting "old" is a persona that some people adopt and some people don't. If we give up learning or trying new things, exercising our creative expression, and closing our minds to new ideas and the possibility that we may change, then we are growing old no matter our age. But those of us who continue these practices whether we're twenty-eight or eighty-two have found a magical elixir, for sure.

TODAY'S ACTION

Pay attention to the youthful qualities in the people around you. Maybe it's their laughter and silliness, their energy and exuberance, or their willingness to try new things. Then try boosting what you find in yourself, and awaken your own inner fountain.

Creation and destruction are the two ends of the
same moment. And everything between the creation
and the next destruction is the journey of life.
—Amish Tripathi

While our current journey of life began with the creation of our physical body and will end with the destruction of its form, physics tells us that the energy that gives life to our bodies can be neither created nor destroyed. In fact, there has never been any more or less energy on this planet than there is right now. The same is true for the elements, like water. Water never goes away; it just changes from solid to liquid to gas over and over again, and moves around the planet. When we understand that nothing ever goes anywhere, but rather is continuously created and destroyed, birthed and rebirthed, we can loosen our fear and attempts to control creation and destruction, and instead tune into the journey between them.

TODAY'S MANTRA

I honor the miracle of each moment between this body's creation and destruction.

Happiness is not something you postpone for the future;
it is something you design for the present.
—Jim Rohn

How often in your past have you put off happiness with the idea that you will only attain it once you reach some future milestone? *I'll be happy when I get that job, when I get the raise, when I have kids, when I have a romantic partner . . .* So often we postpone happiness in the moment because we feel like we need to have or do certain things in order to be happy. But happiness is *here* and *now*, and it is available to you at any time. You can be happy in the midst of struggle, in the process of change, and in the release of calm. You don't need to have any accomplishments or achievements or milestones to have it; happiness is always available.

TODAY'S ACTION

Think of a goal that you have told yourself will make you happier than you are right now. *I'll be happy when I'm not so busy, I'll be happy when I'm not at work*, etc. Flip the script and juice up the drama a little, so that you can see how ridiculous this really sounds: *I'll never be happy until I have nothing to keep me busy at all. I can't possibly find happiness, not even a moment, at work.* May all beings be happy, and this includes you.

You cannot discover new oceans unless you
have the courage to lose sight of the shore.
—André Gide

I s there an area in your life where you are settling for less than the best because it's comfortable or familiar? This doesn't just apply to major life situations, like a relationship or career; it can also apply to your simple day-to-day activities. If something doesn't make your heart sing, why not try doing something else? Making a change can be hard, and it might ding your sense of who you are in the world for a while, but growth means leaving behind the shore of what is familiar and striking out into uncharted waters.

TODAY'S ACTION

You've likely done it at least once today—chosen something comfortable over something new. Go back and redo that decision. Have the tough conversation you walked away from. Change your routine by going to a new grocery store, eating dinner for breakfast, or listening to a radio station you would never think to play.

Silences make the real conversations between friends.
Not the saying but the never needing to say is what counts.
—Margaret Lee Runbeck

Have you ever felt a connection with another being so deep that you can communicate without words? I find this happens most often in small and seemingly innocuous moments; like when my mouth is full but I want to tell my best friend something, and she bursts out laughing at the funny thing I wanted to share with her. Or when I pick up the phone to call a friend and she exclaims on the other end, "I was *just* thinking about you!" Beyond reading one another's minds, deep friendships also are about allowing for silence. When one of us needs support, there doesn't always have to be a long conversation about what's going on and how to fix it; many times being there for someone in silence is the best medicine.

TODAY'S ACTION

Say less today. Try to make space for silence as a tool today by not adding unnecessary words or stories to your conversations. Lean into silence with others, and find your comfort zone there. Silence is a language in and of itself.

Most of us would be upset if we were accused of being "silly." But the word "silly" comes from the old English word selig, and its literal definition is "to be blessed, happy, healthy and prosperous."
—Zig Ziglar

It is not an accident that the first card in a traditional tarot deck is called the Fool. A popular image on many decks finds the Fool smiling while stepping blithely off a cliff. Sometimes being silly or playful can feel like stepping off cliff . . . *What if no one takes me seriously? What if I have fun and then make a big mistake because I'm not paying attention? What if . . .* We get so focused on avoiding any and all potential cliffs that we stay stuck, standing rigidly miles from any edge in our lives. Alternatively, we can get so focused on work, school, and responsibilities (including self-help or spiritual practices) that we forget the importance of having fun. In fact, being silly, playful, and having fun can bring as many blessings and as much happiness, health, and prosperity into our lives as any other practice.

TODAY'S ACTION

Take some time to have *fun* today! Be foolish and celebrate silliness with yourself and those around you.

Imagination and invention go hand in hand.
Remember how lack of resources was never a problem
in childhood games? Shift a few pieces of furniture
around the living room, and you have yourself a fort.
—Alexandra Adornetto

As adults we can get stuck in a mentality of scarcity, springing from the belief that there are not enough material resources or stores of time, love, or friendship for everyone. If we believe this without question, it can become a subtle thread in the background story of our lives. It can lead to jealousy, hoarding of resources, or—most devastating—a loss of imagination. The truth is that we always have exactly what we need, even if we don't always have what we want.

TODAY'S ACTION

Take a moment to show gratitude for all the resources supporting you in this moment, be they material possessions, relationships, or your own inner wisdom.

A quarrel between friends, when made up,
adds a new tie to friendship.
—Saint Francis de Sales

We all have disagreements from time to time with our friends and loved ones. These can be disheartening, scary, or even painful, depending on how deep they cut. But they can also be enormous opportunities for growth. We may have a chance to admit we were wrong, inconsiderate, or mean—which can be hard to admit to anyone, let alone to a good friend who we always want to think the best of us. It may also be a chance to clarify your values and boundaries within a relationship. Either way, by opening up and sharing your vulnerability with those that you're close to, you can strengthen the bonds of friendship. In this way, fighting with friends allows us the opportunity to make up with them in a compassionate and truthful way, which can bring greater depth to our relationship.

TODAY'S ACTION

Can you think of a time you've been wrong or inconsiderate in a friendship? Is there something you can do to strengthen the bond with this person? You might be surprised—sometimes even just a small gesture of outreach is enough to "add a new tie."

The key to developing the courage to change
is to first accept that change is inevitable.
—Wallace Nesbitt

L ife is like a river that constantly flows; and no matter how much we may want to stop time, the waters of each day keep moving. When our internal thoughts sound like: *I want things to stay the same, I like what's familiar,* or *I wish I could go back in time,* then we are creating a subtle backdrop of suffering, because that's not reality. Noticing these thoughts and their connection to how they make us feel is key to allowing them to pass like leaves in a flowing stream rather than attaching and clinging to them. When you feel yourself holding on to the idea that things shouldn't change, you can begin to reform your mind by stating these thoughts to yourself instead: *I embrace the mystery, life is an ever-changing adventure,* and *I'm curious about what's coming next.* As you do, you develop a courageous attitude, and your outlook muscles will grow stronger.

TODAY'S MANTRA

I embrace the magic of change. I look forward to seeing what comes next.

Some people go to priests; others to poetry; I to my friends.
—Virginia Woolf

Friendship offers us innumerable gifts. The presence of our friends makes us feel safe and at ease, joyful, connected, and understood. Being with friends can change a bad day into a good one, a terrible situation into a chance to reconnect, a burden into something far lighter and easier to carry. In the modern world, our friends often constitute what Buddhism calls our sangha, a group of fellow practitioners on our path. In Buddhism, the sangha is just as important as the teachings (dharma) and the example that inner peace is possible (the Buddha). So from a Buddhist perspective, cultivating our relationships with our friends is one of the keys to a happy life.

TODAY'S ACTION

Take an action today to show your friends your gratitude for their presence in your life. Write them a letter or make them a card, invite them out to coffee, or simply call or text them, so that they can hear the sincerity in your voice when you say "thank you for being my friend."

The biggest challenge is to stay focused. It's to have the
discipline when there are so many competing things.
—Alexa Hirschfeld

Discipline is the cornerstone of many religious practices. But some modern spiritual circles shy away from insisting on it, or even valuing it. Maybe this is for fear of seeming too rigid or limiting the freedom of spiritual expression. While I have no interest in donning a nun's habit and a hefty schedule of prayers, I do believe that as we change our lives and develop new and healthy habits, we need repetition to strengthen them. Discipline can be so powerful: it brings our attention to taking action no matter what, and it trains the body to favor the long arc of wellness over the short-term gains of doing whatever we want. If you are in resistance to something that you know is in your best interest, don't think about it—just take action. Then repeat.

TODAY'S ACTION

What new action can you put in place today that will bring more steadiness into your life? Pick one little thing you will do each day and get steady. Rinse and repeat.

To succeed in life, you need three things:
a wishbone, a backbone and a funny bone.
—Reba McEntire

I cannot overstate how important these three "bones" are: the ability to imagine, to stand up for yourself, and to laugh. Having a wishbone allows you to dream. Through your dreams you co-create what is on this planet. Having a backbone doesn't mean you have to be completely armored or untouchable; it only means that you respect yourself enough not to enter into or stay in situations that are harmful to your well-being. And the funny bone keeps your spirits lifted and allows you to find joy in dark days, and silver linings in black clouds.

TODAY'S ACTION

Make three index cards—one for each key idea: wishbone, backbone, and funny bone. Whenever you're feeling stuck, pick one at random. Whether it's wishbone, backbone, or funny bone, take note of the events in that day when you have exercised this particular bone. Have you allowed yourself to dream, or held yourself in high regard, or just flat out laughed? If not, get to it!

*At the worst, a house unkempt cannot
be so distressing as a life unlived.*
—Rose Macaulay

Have you ever felt that you needed to make yourself small, quieter, or less vibrant? That you are "too big," "too loud," or "too much"?

Masks bring our messiness to heel; they hide our beautiful complexity. And this is fine short term if we know what we're doing—say with members of your family who have different worldviews than you, or in an office environment, or even just out grocery shopping. Wearing a mask can help accomplish specific goals (such as at work), but remember these masks are tools, and you can and must remove them when the need for them has passed. Because the mask is fixed, it cannot hold a candle to the real you. So for the big work of life: falling in love, taking risks, learning new skills, and opening new horizons, set the mask aside.

TODAY'S MANTRA

My masks are tools that I use with consciousness and awareness. I can change the tool or remove the mask anytime I need to.

Anything you want to ask a teacher, ask yourself,
and wait for the answer in silence.
—Byron Katie

We all have so much wisdom within us. And yet all of us have found ourselves thinking at one time or another that others are smarter, or more spiritual, or more connected than we are. While there is plenty to learn in the world from many incredible teachers, each time we go outside of ourselves thinking someone else has all the answers, we miss an opportunity to tap into our inner knowing. So yes, we need and benefit from having guides from time to time; but we also want to take the time to patiently tune into our peaceful inner voice for answers. Turning inward might prove to be a longer journey than getting a quick response from someone else, but the knowledge will be more lasting and transformative.

TODAY'S ACTION

Is there a decision you need to make in your life? Instead of immediately asking anyone else's opinion, sit with your question all day. Let it simmer inside and then allow the answer to bubble up from deep within you.

Food for the body is not enough.
There must be food for the soul.
—Dorothy Day

Between work or school, family, friends, household chores, and everything else that we try to fit in in just twenty-four hours, sometimes it can feel like life is a grind, a repetitive cycle without any relief. This is what happens when we attend only to the needs of the physical world, without taking time to truly feed our souls. There are so many ways to feed your soul: a creative expression such as painting, sculpting, or sewing, or simply reconnecting with a pleasure you don't often get, like a long hike or even mindfully indulging in a cupcake from your favorite bakery. Make sure that you aren't simply running from errand to errand without a chance to actually enjoy yourself. Your soul needs to be fed too!

TODAY'S ACTION

Take time out of your day to nourish your soul. Try enjoying a long soak in the tub, pulling out that sketchbook you haven't looked at in a while, playing a neglected instrument, or simply laying out in the sun (don't forget the sunscreen). Make these soul-nourishing activities regular occurrences in your week.

Anxiety is love's greatest killer. It makes others feel as you might when a drowning man holds on to you. You want to save him, but you know he will strangle you with his panic.

—Anaïs Nin

Have you ever felt that anxious sense of *Do they love me? Do they not love me? Will this situation work out how I want it to?* That nervous energy that asks questions out of fear drains our peaceful presence—fast. I've found the cure for when I get anxious and grabby is to look myself in the mirror and say, "Sweetheart, I love you, and you've got this. You are okay. I also love the anxiety that you are feeling right now." That last part is the secret. While anxiety is love's greatest killer, the opposite is also true: love is anxiety's greatest killer. So love that anxiety and watch it transform.

TODAY'S ACTION

Can you love any anxiety or fear when it arises? Fighting your fears gives them power, because the energy of fight *is* the energy of fear. Loving your fears is the path to dissolving them, because love is what shows you there is nothing to be afraid of.

Your own words are the bricks and mortar of the
dreams you want to realize. Your words are the
greatest power you have. The words you choose and
their use establish the life you experience.
—Sonia Choquette

I magine your inner self is like a house. Think about the materials that form the foundation of your soul's home. If the bricks and mortar of your foundation are made of self-judgment, your house will not be sturdy, nor will it be a peaceful place to live. Now imagine that your house is cemented and bricked together with extra-strength self-love as the main ingredient. These walls stand strong and resilient, for self-love is the mortar that can weather the windstorms of life. Many of us tell our loved ones that we love them every day, many times a day. But do we speak those same words to ourselves? Do we lay a sturdy foundation of love, and build from there? It's never too late to start.

TODAY'S ACTION

Find a mirror, look into your eyes, and say, "I love you. You are perfect just the way you are. You deserve to experience good in all its forms."

Let us learn to appreciate there will be times when the trees will
be bare, and look forward to the time when we may pick the fruit.
—Anton Chekhov

Each of us will come across many "winters" in our lives, periods where things can seem dark or cold, when some of the branches that support our lives seem to go barren. Rather than resist these times, the Warrior Goddess path invites us to see them as opportunities to rest and reflect. Observing the cyclical nature of the seasons helps us to remember that our journey flows in circles as well.

TODAY'S ACTION

Are you experiencing a winter in any part of your life? It could be in finances, relationships, or physical or spiritual health. Rather than spend a lot of energy fighting this season, see if you can use this time for rest and reflection. Many problems in our lives take care of themselves if we let them.

The single story creates stereotypes, and the problem with stereotypes is not that they are untrue, but that they are incomplete. They make one story become the only story.
—Chimamanda Ngozi Adichie

Each human has a different point of view, a different background, a different story. When we try to force our own story onto others, or refuse to allow that their experience may be radically different from ours, we miss an opportunity to learn, to connect, and to be whole. To come back into wholeness, both within ourselves and in our communities, we need to step back from our single story and embrace the many stories of the beloveds and strangers around us.

TODAY'S ACTION

Step out of your story completely today and focus on the perspective of others. What is the story of your child? What is the story of your grandparent? What is the story of the person you disagree with? Be with the stories of others as much as possible today, and listen and learn with an open heart. When you step back into your own story, remember to take some of these perspectives with you.

Words are free. It's how you use them that may cost you.
—Rev. J. Martin

We may think our thoughts shape our language, and they do, but it is just as true that our language shapes our thoughts. When we use negative language, our thoughts run further into negative territory. When we instead use positive language, we can encourage more positivity in our thoughts and our overall being. It may be tricky at first, but if you start to change your language, a change in the pattern of your thoughts will follow. Your positive language will also likely rub off on those around you, as we tend to mirror one another energetically. In this way, you will begin putting positivity out into the universe by speaking with positive words. This positivity will then flow back to you, in a blessed circle.

TODAY'S ACTION

Try to spend one day without uttering any negative judgments or complaints. If you catch yourself in one, don't give up for the day. Just notice it and resume the practice.

*You don't start out writing good stuff. You start out
writing crap and thinking it's good stuff, and then
gradually you get better at it. That's why I say one of
the most valuable traits is persistence.*

—Octavia E. Butler

We all want to create masterpieces the first time we try something new. But it's only in accepting those early rough and unpolished edges that allows them to be smoothed as you become more skilled. Persistence will get you through the muddy, crowded terrain until your voice and feet create a smooth path that holds you gently; a path that others can also walk, inspired by your courage and tenacity.

TODAY'S ACTION

Is there a creative process you've been putting off because you're afraid of doing it wrong, because you're ashamed of your skill level, or because your expectations are set on "perfection"? Pretend you are a kid again with a new box of crayons. Be creative. Be messy. Feel the joy of coloring outside the lines. Being creative is one of the most forgotten keys of a happy and meaningful life.

You don't have to control your thoughts.
You just have to stop letting them control you.
—Dan Millman

The belief that we can control our thoughts, or stop the voices in our head, is a little bit like saying we can control a river. We might be able to dam it up for a bit, but it will take up an awful lot of time and energy, and that water will eventually break through. Instead of trying to control or fix your thoughts, try not to take them so seriously instead. Not everything you think is true.

TODAY'S ACTION

Take a few minutes to meditate today, and pay attention to the silent spaces between your thoughts. Even if it's only a half a second in between words in a steady stream of consciousness, there it is. *You*, apart from your thinking mind. I love this exercise because it becomes so clear that we are not our thoughts, or the voice in our head. If we were, we would disintegrate in that little pause between thoughts. Phew! The world doesn't end when we don't believe everything our brain tells us (despite its insistence).

Walk, run, cycle: When you live inside your head for such long periods of time, you have to open the windows, air it out a bit, let sunlight stream into all the dark and dusty corners of your mind.
—Twinkle Khanna

More and more of us are spending time on electronic devices than ever before. I read recently that it is quickly becoming common to spend twelve hours a day plugged into our electronic devices, between computers, phones, television, etc. This means if you sleep for eight hours a day, you spend only four or so hours a day free of an electronic appendage. But what's common is not necessarily normal, or healthy. We should all work to clear some more space to be away from screens. Our brains need sunlight and natural stimulation from the wide world, lest they become stuck in the narrow confines of our electronics. What can you do to unplug, and air out your mind?

TODAY'S ACTION

Notice today how electronic devices take you out of the present moment. Take some time to unplug from all electronics. Go for a walk in the park. Stare out the window. Play a musical instrument. Do nothing. Imagine sunlight streaming into every cell of your body, revitalizing you from the inside out.

The most terrifying thing is to accept oneself completely.
—Carl Jung

Let's start a revolution . . . within. There is nothing more powerful than the force of love. Any human who loves and accepts herself wholeheartedly cannot help but become a potent catalyst for transformation for those around her. Why is self-love so revolutionary? Because it undermines the foundation of so many of the controlling structures we live within. For virtually every human on the planet suffers from the mistaken belief that "I am not worthy." This idea has allowed generations of leaders to create systems of oppression and destruction. But quiet, simple self-love will have none of that, and it turns the whole system on its head, returning power to the people in the most direct and revolutionary way possible

TODAY'S ACTION

Start seeing yourself through the eyes of a lover who is wild about you. Fall in love with your inner beauty, your quirkiness, your tenacity—your whole being.

*Don't be afraid to take risks. In risks will come your biggest
opportunities. Be realistic and be prepared for any outcome
while giving your best at whatever you do.*

—Kirthiga Reddy

I've found that when I take risks, the most amazing things happen. But I also have to understand what the consequences might be. When I am considering taking a risk, I first play a game I call Best Case/Worst Case Scenario where I list all the possible outcomes I can think of so I can make an informed decision. I also acknowledge information I can't or won't have access to. By exploring both the best possible outcome and the worst possible outcome, and accepting the limitations of my existing knowledge, I can be mentally prepared, which allows me to surrender, do my best, and have fun leaping.

TODAY'S ACTION

Is there a risk you've been wanting to take but have held back? Gather all the info you have, and then play the Best Case/Worst Case Scenario game. Get excited about what is possible as well as being realistic about what might happen on the downside. Be prepared for any outcome, and then choose your next move.

You've got to learn to leave the table
when love's no longer being served.
—Nina Simone

If a restaurant served you rotten food, you would never go back. If a server ignored you, you would eventually walk out. There are times and places in our life, such as jobs, relationships, or friendships, when love is no longer being served. Is it time to leave the table, dear one?

TODAY'S ACTION

Serve love at your own table. Pull up a chair, sit down, and take in the nourishment of your own self-respect, self-care, and self-love. When you are providing love to yourself, it becomes much easier to see when others are not.

After the homework is done, trust your instincts.
—Marife Zamora

I had a boss once who was a wonderful role model for using intuition within the context of business. She was a very successful businesswoman who knew the ins and outs of marketing, how to read profit and loss statements, and where she wanted to take her company. But at the end of the day, after she had made use of all of the traditional business tools at her disposal, she would set aside time to get quiet so that she could *feel into* what her next best business decision needed to be. Very boldly, she allowed her gut to have the final say, not reason or intellect. She wasn't always able to back up her final decisions with logic, or explain to others why she made one choice over another, but her success was undeniable.

TODAY'S ACTION

When you have a decision to make, it's important to do the pragmatic homework. Then throw it all out and see where your instincts guide you when you simply listen.

Do what you can in the time that
you have, in the place where you are.
—Shirley S. Raguindin

I remember telling a couple of friends about a fabulous exotic place that I was about to travel to, and one friend's response in particular gave me pause. Others had told me they were jealous, or shared a place that they had always longed to go. This one friend wished me well on my journey with a warm and open heart, and indicated the absolute peace and tranquility he felt in his own life as it was. He was happy for my adventures, but content with his own life without seeking outside of himself. There was no longing or desire, just a beautiful appreciation for my journey and a radical acceptance of his life choices. When we accept the time that we have in the place we are at, we can enjoy what we have. There is no need to be someplace else or someone else; the current moment is perfect.

TODAY'S ACTION

Practice resting into exactly the place and the being that you are. Imagine placing yourself on a map that represents your life and draw a small circle around you. Discover the actions you can take that will be of benefit to those who are within your small sphere of influence.

Some of us have great runways already built for us. If
you have one, take off. But if you don't have one, realize
it is your responsibility to grab a shovel and build one for
yourself and for those who will follow after you.
—Amelia Earhart

Whether your path has been smoothed by those who have walked before you, or you're carving out your own path . . . there is work to do. Thank those who have carved whatever path they could for you, and then take your next step. If that path leads away from the direction you want to go, gather your tools and start making a trail that is uniquely yours. You are within a continuum, and your hard work will leave a legacy for others. What opportunities do you want to leave for those who come after you?

TODAY'S ACTION

Take some time to look at your life from a vast sky view. Are you carving a new trail, or following the trail of those who have walked before you? Imagine the gifts you want to leave for those who will follow on your path.

We wear clothes, and speak, and create civilizations, and believe we are more than wolves. But inside us there is a word we cannot pronounce and that is who we are.

—Anthony Marra

Underneath the clothes, language, and trappings of human society, we are both animal and spiritual. When we stop identifying as solely human, and embrace both our wild animal and our expansive spirit, we move beyond language and thought. In this realm of truth, we face the raw, wordless beauty that we are.

TODAY'S ACTION

Today let go of some of your human-ness to engage and listen to the wise silence of your being-ness.

You can have fantasies about having control over the world, but I know I can barely control my kitchen sink. That is the grace I'm given. Because when one can control things, one is limited to one's own vision.

—Kiki Smith

Believing we have the capacity (or the mission) to control people, places, or things may feel powerful in the short run, but in the long run it always proves damaging, frustrating, and ultimately unfulfilling. Any fix we have made by forcing our will on a situation is temporary and limited, and we have closed ourselves off to the wisdom of the universe. Try on these words instead: *Guide. Steward. Invite. Nourish. Connect.* Today, explore how you might open to bigger possibilities by surrendering control in some area of your life and inviting in a larger vision.

TODAY'S MANTRA

Guide. Steward. Invite. Nourish. Connect.

I knew that if I allowed fear to overtake me, my journey was doomed. Fear, to a great extent, is born of a story we tell ourselves, and so I chose to tell myself a different story from the one women are told. I decided I was safe. I was strong. I was brave. Nothing could vanquish me.

—Cheryl Strayed

Think of a time, perhaps outside looking at the stars on a summer night, surrounded by the dark, when you felt nurtured, protected, and strong. Now call to mind a time you were terrified outside at night, even though there was no immediate threat. What was different? Probably the story you told yourself, or one an older sibling told you to mess with your head. The point is, believe a different story about the same scenario, and you will find an infinite range of experience. What story have you told yourself that keeps you from connecting with the wildness of nature? What fears limit the wildness of your expression? What doubts keep you from walking wild new trails? We can always—*always*—tell ourselves a different story.

TODAY'S ACTION

Today turn toward the wild: spend time alone in nature or plan a journey to the beach or the mountains. Be wildly brave.

ABOUT THE AUTHOR

HeatherAsh Amara brings an openhearted, inclusive worldview to her writings and teachings, which are a rich blend of Toltec wisdom, European shamanism, Buddhism, and Native American ceremony. She is the author of *Warrior Goddess Training*, *The Warrior Goddess Way*, and numerous other books. Visit her at www.heatherashamara.com.

Hier◉phantpublishing

books that inspire your body, mind, and spirit

Hierophant Publishing
8301 Broadway, Suite 219
San Antonio, TX 78209
888-800-4240

www.hierophantpublishing.com